SWEDISH COOKING

ICA Test Kitchen
ICA provkök

ICA bokförlag Västerås

Coverphotos: Front, gravlax with gravlax sauce, recipes on page 77. Back, Christmas Eve smörgåsbord.

© 1983 ICA-förlaget AB, Västerås
8th edition
First edition published 1971

Recipes selected by ICA provkök (ICA Test Kitchen)
Text and translation: Görel Kristina Näslund
Cover and book design: Ulf Lindahl
Photographs: Ulf Christer, Hans B. Eriksson, Björn Lindberg, Olle Åkerström
Printed in Sweden by Ljungföretagen, Örebro, 1984

ISBN 91-534-0823-3

Contents

Foreword

Visiting a foreign country — either for a short or long time — you soon notice that lots of things are different from what you are used to. Foods and eating habits for example, differ quite a bit from country to country.

Cooking in a foreign country with new foreign foods can be an exciting adventure. It is fun to try the specialties of the country in one's own kitchen. Or just to read about what goes into the new dishes one meets.

This book is meant as a guide to Swedish food today. "Swedish Cooking" gives more than a hundred recipes characteristic of Swedish food, both the everyday kind and the more festive fare. To make it easier to use the recipes, the ingredients are given in ounces and cups as well as in grams and deciliters.

Brown beans, pea soup and many other traditional Swedish *husmanskost* dishes take a long time to prepare. You can now buy these dishes ready-cooked in the supermarkets.

Good food, plenty of good food, has always been part of Swedish holiday celebrations. In this matter, Swedes are very tradition-bound. Everyone must have *lutfisk* on Christmas Eve. Or Fat Tuesday Buns during Lent and gaily colored eggs at Easter. Many dishes, such as cheese cake, potato dumplings and *glödhoppa,* are typical of a special province. The book will tell you more about all this.

Going to a Swedish dinner party may bring on problems for the uninitiated guest from another country. The chapter on Swedish etiquette gives you some good advice how to be a guest and how to be a host or hostess in Sweden. You will also find here the rules for how to handle the *smörgåsbord.* Finally, the book leaves you a few menus for typical Swedish meals, both everyday family meals and more festive meals. The recipes for the dishes suggested in these menus are all included in the book.

Swedish Food Traditions

G enuine Swedish food — is there such a thing? Tournedos, paella, hamburgers... the food served in Swedish homes and restaurants often has a foreign flavor as a result of the Swedish love of travel.

But Sweden does indeed have a fine old culinary tradition rich in native dishes. The Swedish *husmanskost,* good old everyday Swedish food based on classic country cooking, has admittedly been influenced by foreign cuisine over the years. Basically, however, it is genuinely Swedish.

Today, the plain and hearty husmanskost is undergoing a renaissance in Sweden. The best of the old recipes have been revived and often revised so that they are less sturdy, simpler to prepare and better suited to the modern way of living without having lost any of their special charm and characteristics. Propaganda for better diets has also helped to improve the Swedish husmanskost by a reduction of the fat content matched by an addition of fresh fruit and vegetables.

The Swedish Smörgåsbord

The Swedish *smörgåsbord* is world famous. Today, however, the traditional large smörgåsbord with its lavish array of food can be found only in a few restaurants, usually at Christmas time. A much reduced version of the smörgåsbord is sometimes served in the home, also usually at Christmas time. Once in a while, mostly in rural areas, the complete old-time smörgåsbord will be prepared. When you meet with a smörgåsbord of this kind, it is important to know the rules for how to approach it, or it may become just a hotchpotch of flavors and impressions.

The commonly accepted and best way of enjoying the large smörgåsbord is to eat each kind of food separately, changing to a clean plate whenever it is deemed necessary. Never try to sample everything but take a little of each of your favorite dishes. Start with the herring and let it be accompanied by a potato, crispbread and butter. When you have relished this, go back for some smoked, pickled or poached fish. Return to the smörgåsbord and help yourself to your favorites among the cold cuts and salads. Then sample the hot dishes. Finally have some cheese and fruit and, if desired, dessert and coffee. Remember that you are free to take as many trips to the smörgåsbord as you want to, but never load your plate with too many various foods at the same time.

A small smörgåsbord consisting of a few herring dishes, hot boiled potatoes, butter, cheese and crispbread is often served as an appetizer before dinner. Sometimes this smörgåsbord may be extended with a few more dishes and served for a late supper. A medium large smörgåsbord is often a practical form of buffet-style entertaining. In the chapter on menus you will find suggestions for a smörgåsbord.

The Swedish Sandwich

Bread, butter and cheese are often served with the meal in Sweden. Everyone makes his own open-faced sandwich which is eaten whole, either before, during or at the end of the meal — the sandwich is not broken or cut in pieces. Foreigners in Sweden are often astonished to see large sandwiches being eaten out of the hand without using a knife and fork, but this is the fully accepted way of eating any sandwich so prepared to make it practical.

Danish style sandwiches or *smörrebröd* consisting of a single thin slice of bread generously covered with meat, fish or cheese and appropriate garnish are quite popular in Sweden; served on festive occasions, this kind of sandwiches are always eaten with a knife and fork.

For a large part of the Swedish people, sandwiches often make the whole lunch or supper. The ingredients may then be served separately or as ready-made sandwiches. For the everyday sandwich, crispbread is a must. This Swedish specialty comes in different shapes, from the large round type with or without a hole in the center to the smaller oblong pieces; and in various thicknesses, from the coarse thick rye crispbread to the thin white and brittle Norrland crispbread.

The once so popular sweet *limpa* is slowly being replaced by more wholesome unsweetened bread. Sour dough bread baked of wholemeal, dark rye or barley flour tastes wonderful together with good cheese and sausage, the two most common toppings for Swedish sandwiches.

The Swedish cheese industry offers good reproductions of foreign cheeses as well as a number of excellent native specialties. Here are the names of the most popular Swedish cheeses.

Grevé resembles Swiss cheese with its sweet mild flavor.

Herrgårdsost is usually sold aged. Fresh it has a mild round flavor.

Hushållsost is a typical Swedish "country cheese" with a mild, slightly sour taste.

Kryddost is flavored with caraway and cloves.

Mesost is made from the whey obtained at cheese making. Brown, quite sweet. Children like it.

Prästost is a fine old Swedish cheese with quite a strong flavor when well aged.

Sveciaost is the best selling cheese in Sweden. Fresh it has a mild flavor, when aged the taste becomes strong and sharp. Sometimes flavored with cloves and caraway.

Västerbottenost a juicy brittle cheese common on the smörgåsbord. When aged, its flavor is strong and sharp.

There are also many kinds of good Swedish sausages well worth trying. Very few today make their own sausage but many of the old provincial recipes are used by the meat packing plants and good sausages can be bought every where. Especially the juniper-smoked and sauna-smoked sausages have a rich flavor and are very popular. The following smoked sausages all make good toppings for sandwiches.

Femmarkerkorv has a hearty, slightly sour flavor.

Spickekorv resembles salami sausage but is saltier and includes onion.

Herrgårdskorv or **dalarökorv** has a rich, slightly sour flavor.

Boiled **medwurst** and **skinkwurst,** with pieces of cooked ham, also make good sandwich toppings.

Food and Festivals in Sweden

Christmas

Slaughtering, beer brewing, cooking, baking, candle making — these were some of the holiday preparations common in the old rural household. Today most Swedes lead a comfortable urban life and practically the entire Christmas holiday fare may be bought ready-made at the store.

Nevertheless, come December and a smell of cinnamon and saffron, candles and copper polish can be noticed in every Swedish home. At no other time do the Swedes take so much trouble in preserving old customs as at *jul* and to do some of your own cooking and baking is part of the holiday fun.

Julafton, Christmas Eve, is the all-important day of feasting and gift-giving. Usually around 2 p.m. Christmas lunch will be served in the kitchen buffet-style. Once a lavish table crowded with

A Christmas Eve buffet-style smörgåsbord with some of the traditional Christmas dishes; glassblower's herring, herring salad, liver paté, ovenbaked Christmas ham, jellied veal, pork sausage, smoked sausage and red cabbage salad.

14

heavy dishes hot and cold, this Christmas Eve smörgåsbord is now considerably cut down in size to better suit the modern way of living.

One old-time dish, however, the Christmas ham, will probably always remain a part of the holiday fare. Many Swedes also insist on *dopp i grytan* or Dip in the Pot for a complete Christmas Eve: slices of rye bread are immersed in hot bouillon and then enjoyed together with ham, pork sausage or butter. Beer is the common beverage with the smörgåsbord which usually ends with coffee and Christmas cookies.

After lunch begins the wait for *tomten*, the Swedish Santa Claus and gift-bringer. When tomten has left and all the presents have been opened and admired, it is time for the traditional julafton supper — *lutfisk* and creamed rice. The custom of eating lutfisk, dried codfish cured with lye, is said to date from the time when Sweden was a Catholic country.

An old custom is to use the creamed rice as a means of divination. Hide a blanched almond in it — the recipient will marry within the coming year. Add a bitter almond — spinsterhood is in store for you. A small shiny coin — you are sure to become rich. Tradition requires everyone to produce a poem before approaching the creamed rice; it does not have to have high literary pretensions but it must be original.

Christmas Eve Smörgåsbord

Glassblower's Herring p. 64
with Boiled Potatoes
Herring Salad p. 49
Jellied Veal p. 99
Pork Roll p. 98
Spare Ribs p. 99
Meatballs p. 85
Liver Pâté p. 100
Ovenbaked Christmas Ham p. 98
Red Cabbage Salad p. 52
Bread, Butter, Cheese
Coffee with Almond Tarts p. 112
or Ginger Snaps p. 114

Christmas Eve Supper

Lutfisk with Lutfisk Sauce p. 83
Boiled Potatoes and Green Peas
Creamed Rice with Milk p. 117

Lent

Converting the Nordic people to Christianity was
not an easy task for the French monks and English
missionaries sent to Scandinavia around the year
1000. For one thing, the people could not under-
stand the necessity of fasting during Lent, the
forty-day period of quiet and abstinence decreed
by the Catholic Church. Legend has it that the
Vikings grumbled, clanked their swords and be-
haved on the whole in such a threatening manner
that the authorities found it best to ease the
regulations and allow the people a hearty meal of
salt pork every Tuesday.

It is now more than 400 years since Sweden
converted to the Protestant Church but the tradition of having a heavy meal on Tuesdays during
Lent is still observed. Fried salt pork with brown
beans is the customary fare followed by a sturdy
dessert called Fat Tuesday Buns, wheat-flour buns
filled with almond paste, topped with whipped
cream and served floating in a bowl of hot milk.

Lady Day

A survivor from Catholic times, Lady Day or
Annunciation Day, remained a legal holiday on the
Swedish calendar until 1952. Since then, Lady
Day has been observed on the Sunday closest to

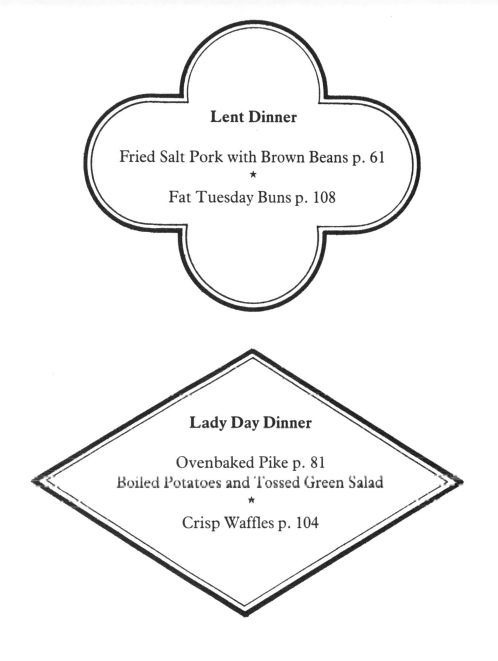

Lent Dinner

Fried Salt Pork with Brown Beans p. 61
★
Fat Tuesday Buns p. 108

Lady Day Dinner

Ovenbaked Pike p. 81
Boiled Potatoes and Tossed Green Salad
★
Crisp Waffles p. 104

19

the old date, March 25th. Through dialectic corruption, the old Swedish name for Lady Day, *Vårfrudagen* became *Våfferdagen* and later *Våffeldagen* meaning Waffle Day. Thus was born the custom of having waffles for dessert on Lady Day.

Easter

Easter holiday means sunshine, snow, skiing, tulips, daffodils and budding birch twigs adorned with multicolored feathers. Easter is also litte girls dressed as witches, a reminder of former times when the holiday was marked by a strong belief in dark superstitions. In the old days, Easter week even called for a special menu that included kale soup on Maundy Thursday, salt salmon pudding on Good Friday, and boiled eggs on Easter Eve.

Today there are no set rules, but Easter Eve most Swedes will have a small smörgåsbord and boiled colored eggs are seldom missing. The Easter Sunday menu often includes a green soup and a pork or lamb roast.

Midsummer

To Swedes from time immemorial, Midsummer has always been a very special festival — a joyous

Easter Sunday Dinner

Nettle or Spinach Soup p. 56
Roast Lamb p. 93
Hasselback Potatoes p. 60 and Tossed Green Salad
★

Vanilla Ice Cream with Cloudberry Preserve

Midsummer Day Dinner

Smoked Warm Salmon Trout p. 78 or
Gravlax with Gravlax Sauce p. 77
★

Fried Chicken p. 97
Boiled New Potatoes
Tossed Green Salad or Mushroom Salad p. 49
★

Fresh Strawberries with Whipped Cream

celebration of summer, sunshine, youth and love. If you want to meet the magic of the Nordic summer, go out into the country on Midsummer Eve. Join in the medieval ring dances around the Maypole, a tall mast covered with garlands of fresh wild flowers and birch twigs. Or just listen to the gay old tunes from fiddle and accordion. Take a walk and breathe in the loveliness of the light summer night. Like everyone else you will forget to go to bed but stay up with the sun throughout the night.

Midsummer Day is usually celebrated with a dinner party outdoors. The traditional Midsummer menu includes salmon, chicken, new potatoes and fresh strawberries.

Crayfish and Surströmming

At the end of the summer, Swedes begin to look forward to the parties given in the honor of two seasonal delicacies — *kräftor* and *surströmming*.

The second Thursday in August is the opening date for *kräftor* or crayfish. The small, black, fresh-water crustaceans are dropped live into boiling salted water with a huge bunch of dill; during cooking the crayfish, like the lobster, change their color to a bright red. After having been chilled for several hours, the crayfish are removed from the cooking liquid and piled in a huge mound on a platter decorated with fresh dill crowns.

Crayfish with fresh dill crowns.

The ritual of crayfish eating is a wonderfully happy, noisy and messy shirt-sleeve affair; large bibs and paper napkins protect the diners as they do their best to suck out every morsel of meat and every drop of juice from the crayfish shell. A full August moon and gay paper lanterns complete the crayfish party which is usually held outdoors.

Surströmming, fermented Baltic herring, is in its own way just as dramatic a delicacy as crayfish. A specialty of northern Sweden, surströmming is for sale beginning the third Thursday in August.

To serve surströmming the proper way, tie a napkin around the can and place it on the table. Then carefully open the can — a strong odor will at once reach your nostrils and fill the room. Neophytes often need some time to get used to the unique smell of surströmming, some even go so far as to call it a stench. To seasoned surströmming lovers, however, nothing smells better than this little fish which is always served with hot boiled potatoes, preferably *mandelpotatis,* the curved, oblong, yellow potatoes grown in northern Sweden.

Thin white crispbread, also a Norrland specialty, butter and chopped onion are the other accompaniments. Many like to make a *klämma* or surströmming sandwich: put butter, sliced potatoes and fillets of surströmming between two pieces of crispbread.

St. Martin's Day

Once upon a time, there was in the French town
Tours a pious monk, called Martin, who was so
much loved by the people that they wanted him to
become their bishop. Martin, however, preferred
to remain a monk and hid from his supporters in a
flock of geese. Unfortunately the startled geese
betrayed Martin by their vociferous gaggling. He
was found and had to surrender. He took his
revenge by deciding that every year on the day of
his betrayal a goose should be killed and cooked for
dinner. Ever since then, November 11th, known
as St. Martin's Day, has been celebrated with a
goose dinner.

A legend is a legend is a legend. Certainly it is
quite a coincidence that just at this time of the year
the goose is nicely fattened and just right to be
slaughtered. The tradition of having a goose dinner
on St. Martin's Day spread north to Denmark and
from there to Skåne, the Swedish province where
people always have had an understanding for good
food.

Today *Mårten Gås* — a festive goose dinner on
Mårtens afton or St. Martin's Eve, November 10th
— is a popular tradition among all Swedes. Still, it
is only in Skåne that school children are given the
day off. In a small family, a duck or a large chicken
may be substituted for the goose, but whatever the
bird, the frame around it is always the same.

An authentic goose dinner starts with *svartsoppa* or black soup, a dark velvety soup made of goose or pig's blood. This soup may be obtained ready-cooked in most grocery stores in November.

Mårten Gås Dinner

Black Soup
★

Roast Goose p. 96
Boiled or Baked Potatoes, Stewed Prunes and
Apples, Red Cabbage p. 61
★

Fresh Fruit

Regional Specialties

O n the whole, Swedes today all have the same food habits and customs. However, many provinces have a reputation for a special food or a local dish that may be prepared in the same way now as it was hundreds of years ago. A trip through Sweden's twenty-four provinces can be an exciting culinary adventure.

Let us start our tour in Skåne, Sweden's southernmost province and the home of festive Mårten Gås dinners, lavish smörgåsbord luncheons and grand *ålagillen* or eel parties serving eel prepared in a dozen different ways.

When in Skåne, remember to sample the *spettekaka*, the classic party cake of the province. Made of eggs, sugar and flour, the batter is slowly dropped onto a cone that rotates over open fire. After baking the tower-like cake is decorated with white frosting and adorned with flowers at the top.

Småland boasts its own famous dessert of nationwide popularity, the *ostkaka* or cheese cake. In the old days, ostkaka was served only on special occasions such as weddings, funerals and important holidays.

The country woman would wrap her ostkaka, made from numerous pints of milk and cream, in her best linen napkin, then wrap herself in her black Sunday silk scarf and be off for the party. Because all the women did the same thing, it could happen that 10 or 12 cheese cakes crowded the kitchen of the hostess. When it was time for dessert, every one of the cheese cakes had to be set out on the table. Good manners required that every guest sampled each ostkaka always starting at the center of the cake. Thus any left-over ostkaka could be filled with cream or fruit and served the following day as a "new" dessert. Today the food industry distributes ostkaka to all parts of the country and it has become an everyday dessert.

Småland and Öland are both known for their *kroppkakor,* dumplings made from raw as well as cooked potatoes, flour and salt. True kroppkakor are filled with cubed salt pork and allspice; boiled in water, they are served steaming hot with lingonberry preserve and melted butter.

On the west coast, Halland and Bohuslän offer a wide variety of fish and shellfish prepared as hearty soups, salads and casseroles.

If potato sausage is your dish, stop in Värmland and sample the true Värmland sausage made with beef, pork and cubed potatoes; when in Dalarna, try the local beef stew called *sö*. But if you are partial to lamb and mutton, go to Gotland and you will be treated to such good native dishes as *glödhoppa* — broiled slices of dried and salted lamb.

Along the coast of the Gulf of Bothnia, from Uppland to Norrbotten, the most important food is *strömming*. This small silvery fish, also called Baltic herring, is prepared with knowing hands into a multitude of different dishes, all delicious.

Good salmon, trout, whitefish and whitefish caviar are other delights waiting for you in Norrland, the nine northern provinces of Sweden.

If you do not love fish, Norrland has still a lot to offer. You must try the dark, gamy reindeer meat from Lappland. Or the Västerbotten cheese, a smörgåsbord favorite. Or *åkerbär*, the rare exquisite berry that grows wild on short-stemmed plants along roadsides and ditches. The åkerbär looks like a small juicy raspberry but has an intensive, delightful aroma all of its own. The *hjortron* or cloudberry is another fine Norrland fruit.

Two Norrland provinces, Västerbotten and Norrbotten, have their own famous dumplings, *palt*. Even more filling than kroppkakor, these dumplings, too, are served with butter and

Traditional dishes from Skåne, smoked eel and spettekaka. The smoked eel is here served with scrambled eggs, a salad and Swedish crisp bread.

lingonberries. To enjoy palt best, do as the natives do; dig a hole in the dumpling and fill with butter. Then cut the palt in small pieces and dip into the well of quickly melting butter.

Other favorite Norrland specialties are *tunn-bröd*, the thin white crispbread, and *fil-* or *långmjölk*. A lightly soured milk product, fil sometimes becomes so thick and "long" that a spoon dipped into it will come out perfectly clean, bright and shiny. Fil and tunnbröd are often combined into an old-time dish called *bryta* — fil mixed with small pieces of tunnbröd. *Blöta* is the cold-weather dish — tunnbröd simmered in beef or pork bouillon and enjoyed hot with boiled pork or pork sausage.

Skål, Tack —
Swedish Customs

S wedes have long had a reputation of being a
stiff and formal people. Formerly, foreigners
travelling in Sweden were often confused by the
ceremonious drinking rituals and protocol of
etiquette. But all this has changed. Modern
Swedes are more and more doing away with the
strict old rules. Extensive travelling has given
them an international outlook and understanding
of customs in other countries. Of course, older
Swedes may still want to adhere to the proper
etiquette and some are hurt when addressed with
an improper *Du* or *Ni*, but, in general, everyone
pays little attention to these things. However, for
you who would like to know what is right
behavior at dinner parties, here are a few things to
remember.

When You are the Guest

Flowers to the hostess are always welcome. On formal occasions, the flowers are sent beforehand or afterwards with a thank-you-note.

After sitting down at the table, and wine has been served, the host makes a short welcome speech and proposes a *skål;* one should not drink before this skål. Afterwards, everyone is free to drink or to propose a skål as often as they wish. It is only at very formal dinner parties that one never drinks except in the form of a skål. When there are more than six people at the table, one must never skål the host and hostess in order to spare them from drinking more than they want to.

This is the ritual of the formal skål. Someone proposes a skål with one or several persons. They all lift their glasses to "the third waistcoat button" and bow to each other, their eyes meeting. One sips the wine and lowers the glass back to the level of that same button while again meeting the eyes of the partner or partners. Another slight bow and the glasses are put back on the table.

Today, a skål is very often accompanied by just a friendly nod and a smile. Naturally, also those who are drinking non-alcoholic beverages may participate in a skål.

When the dessert has been served, the guest sitting to the left of the hostess thanks her for the good food from all of the guests; this may be done in the form of a little speech or simply be a few words of appreciation followed by a proposal of a skål for the host and hostess.

At a small dinner party, instead of a speech, it is customary that everyone personally thanks the host and hostess when the meal is over. Before leaving, one should again thank the host and hostess. If you want to be correct, do this before putting on your coat.

Sometimes during the week after the party, one may thank the host and hostess again by a written note or a telephone call. Although this is no longer a must, it is always nice for the hostess to hear from her guests in some way.

When You are the Host or Hostess

For a formal dinner party, written invitations are sent out at least 14 days beforehand and an answer is requested. In other cases, customs differ; invitations may be written or made over the telephone. Note that in Sweden an invitation is usually taken seriously. It is not as common as in the United States to say "You must come over and have dinner with us" without meaning anything more than a kind phrase.

Place-cards are usually used only on formal occasions; guests are then seated according to age, rank, relationship etc. But very often one simply seats those guests together who are supposed to enjoy each other. The hostess always has the male guest of honor as her partner; his place is to the left of the hostess. The host and his partner, the lady guest of honor, go first to the table while the hostess and her escort wait until last.

It is always nice if the host and hostess skål not only their partners but all of their guests. The guests will also appreciate if besides saying one is happy that they could come, one says thanks for the flowers or whatever the guests brought with them.

Swedish Groceries

Perhaps many will be searching this book for recipes for rose hip soup, liver dumplings or black soup. Why are not these old-time favorites included? The reason is that today these and other good but time-consuming dishes are produced by the Swedish food industry with an excellent result. Much of the good old husmanskost food is available fully or partly prepared; canned, frozen or freeze-dried.

Of course, to some the work preparing a certain favorite dish may be fun even if it takes time. Many times, however, it is a good idea to go half the way, that is, to use the industry product and season it with spices and other additions to suit the personal taste. Or you may cook one dish with great care and buy the rest of the food for the meal ready-made.

Some dishes are, of course, cheaper to make yourself than to buy. The difference is not very

big, however, unless the household is very large.
Today hardly anyone makes everything themselves
– bakes the bread, cooks the preserves etc. Even
if you do not work outside the home, you may
want to use your time for other things than
cooking and baking.

Here follows a list of some common Swedish
groceries.

Svenska specerier	Swedish groceries
bakpulver	baking powder
bruna bönor	brown beans
Bröd	*Bread*
franska	white loaf
kaffebröd, bullar	buns
knäckebröd	crispbread
limpa	rye loaf, rye bread
pepparkakor	ginger snaps
småfranska	rolls
småkakor	cookies
majonnäs	mayonnaise
mandel	almonds
margarin	margarine
Mjöl och gryn	*Meal, flour, cereals*
grahamsmjöl	wholemeal flour
havregryn	porridge oats
havremjöl	oatmeal
korngryn	barley
kornmjöl	barley flour
majsmjöl	cornflour
mannagryn	semolina
matlagningsmjöl	flour
potatismjöl	potato starch flour
risgryn	rice

rågmjöl	rye flour
rågsikt	rye and wheat flour
vetemjöl	all-purpose flour

Mjölk	*Milk*
filmjölk	sour milk
gräddfil	sour cream
kaffegrädde	light cream
lättmjölk	low-fat milk (0.5%)
standardmjölk	whole milk (3%)
vispgrädde	whipping cream

Rökt fisk och fiskkonserver	*Smoked and canned fish*
ansjovisfiléer	anchovy fillets
böckling	smoked Baltic herring
fiskbullar	fish balls
inläggningssill, vattenlagd	soaked salt herring fillets
laxrom	salmon roe
löjrom	whitefish roe
rökt salt kaviar	smoked salt cod roe
salt kaviar	red salt cod roe
salt sill	salt herring
torskrom	cod roe

| senap | mustard |
| smör | butter |

Socker	*Sugar*
bitsocker	lump sugar
farinsocker	brown sugar
florsocker	icing sugar
pärlsocker	crushed sugar
sirap	treacle, syrup
strösocker	castor sugar

ströbröd	bread crumbs
ärtor, gula	dried yellow peas
ägg, stora (gröna)	eggs, big (green marking)
ägg medel (röda)	eggs, medium (red marking)
ägg små (blå)	eggs, small (blue marking)

39

Things to Remember
When Using the Recipes

A ll recipes give 4 servings unless otherwise indicated. All measurements are level.

The measures used in Sweden are liter (l), deciliter (dl), kilogram (kg) and gram (g). The standard set of measuring spoons includes tablespoon, teaspoon and *kryddmått (krm)*or spice spoon. Use the following table to translate Swedish measurements into the nearest convenient American equivalent and vice versa.

---

1 dl = 100 milliliter (ml) or fluid grams = 6⅔ tablespoons = 3½ fluid ounces
1 liter = 10 dl = 1 fluid kilogram (kg) = 2.2 fluid pounds
1 spice spoon = 1 ml
1 teaspoon = 5 ml = ⅙ fluid ounce
1 tablespoon = 15 ml = 3 teaspoons = ½ fluid ounce
1 U.S. cup = 8 fluid ounces = 227 ml or 2.27 dl
1 pound (lb) = 16 ounces (oz) = 454 g
1 ounce = 28.35 g
1000 g = 1 kilogram (kg)

(The British fluid ounce is 1.04 times the American ounce.)

To convert grams to ounces, multiply the grams by 0.035.

Miscellaneous Measures

	1 dl	1 table-spoon
Cocoa	40 g	
Coffee	40 g	
Brown sugar	70 g	
Wholemeal flour	60 g	
Macaroni	50 g	
Margarine and butter, solid		15 g
Margarine and butter, melted	90 g	13 g
Nuts, shelled	65 g	
Oil	90 g	13 g
Oat meal	35 g	
Potato starch flour	80 g	12 g
Icing sugar	60 g	
Raisins	60 g	
Rice	85 g	
Rye flour	55 g	
Salt	125 g	19 g
Sugar	85 g	
Syrup	140 g	
All-purpose flour	60 g	9 g

Flour used in the recipes is always Swedish all-purpose wheat flour except when otherwise indicated.

Swedish spirit vinegar *ättiksprit* (12% acidity), Swedish syrup, lingonberry and cloudberry preserves, potato starch flour, pearl sugar and vanilla sugar may be obtained in Scandinavian delicatessens in the United States.

Always bake in a preheated oven.

Oven Temperatures

All temperatures are stated in ° Celsius (Centigrades).

To convert Celsius into Fahrenheit, multiply by 9, divide by 5, and add 32.

To convert Fahrenheit into Celsius, subtract 32, multiply by 5, and divide by 9.

Conversion Table (rounded figures)

°Celsius	°Fahrenheit	
100 to 150	212 to 300	slow
175 to 225	350 to 425	moderate
250	475	hot
275	525	very hot

Can Sizes

Fish, vegetables, fruit:

$1/1$-can contains about 8 dl = 800 g
$1/2$-can contains about 4 dl = 400 g
$1/4$-can contains about 2 dl = 200 g

Soups:
Soup cans come in two sizes; the family-size can contains about 1 liter, the smaller can about 6 dl.

Meat:
Large $1/2$-can contains about 500 g.
Large $1/3$-can contains about 300 g.
Mushrooms also come in $1/8$-cans which contain about 100 g. Can sizes refer to Swedish standard sizes.

How Much?

Fish
Whole cleaned fish	200 to 250 g per serving
Fish, cut in slices	150 to 200 g per serving
Fish fillets	100 to 150 g per serving

Meat:
Meat on the bone	150 to 250 g per serving
Boneless meat	100 to 150 g per serving
Ground meat	75 to 100 g per serving
Salt pork	75 to 100 g per serving
Bacon	50 to 75 g per serving
Ham, cooked or smoked . . .	75 to 100 g per serving

Miscellaneous:
Cheese for sandwiches	20 g per serving
Cheese for cheeseboard	50 to 100 g per serving
Butter or margarine for the table	10 to 15 g per serving
Creamed or melted butter or margarine	20 to 25 g per serving
Mayonnaise, 1 to 2 table-spoons or	15 to 30 g per serving

Sandwiches

The open-faced Swedish sandwich varies in size from the tiny canapé to the giant many-sectioned sandwich that is a whole meal in itself.

A very Swedish way to start a dinner is with three small sandwiches. Designed to stimulate the appetite this diminutive form of the Swedish smörgåsbord offers a selection of fish, meat and cheese arranged on small pieces of bread cut in various shapes.

Three Small Sandwiches
Tre små smörgåsar

Here follow suggestions how to prepare three small sandwiches; just before the guests sit down, put one sandwich of each kind at each table setting.

Caviar and Egg
Kaviar och ägg

white unsliced sandwich bread
margarine or butter
salt or smoked cod roe caviar
chopped hard-boiled egg
dill

Slice the bread lengthwise and spread with magarine or butter. Trim the crust. Put caviar along the edges and sprinkle with chopped hard-boiled egg in center. Cut across the sandwich strip to make small oblong sandwiches. Garnish with dill sprigs.

Ham and Prunes
Skinka och sviskon

rye bread
margarine or butter
lettuce
sliced ham
pitted prunes
parsley

Slice the bread and cut in triangles. Spread with margarine or butter. Cover with lettuce and top with ham and prunes. Garnish with parsley.

Cheddar and Cucumber
Cheddarost och gurka

white unsliced sandwich bread
   or rye bread
margarine or butter
thick slices cheddar cheese
cucumber

Slice the bread lengthwise and spread with margarine or butter. Cover with cheese and cut out rounds. Garnish with thinly sliced cucumber.

Caviar Canapé
Löjromssnitt

4 slices white sandwich bread
margarine or butter
2 to 3 tablespoons finely chopped chives
50 g (about 2 oz.) whitefish caviar
1 lemon

Trim the crust. Spread the bread with margarine or butter and press into finely chopped chives. Cut in triangles or rounds. Put a small mound of caviar in center of sandwich and garnish with a piece of lemon.

Open-faced sandwiches. From bottom, three small sandwiches, giant gourmet sandwich, caviar canapé, lapp sandwich, herring sandwich and shrimp sandwich.

Shrimp Sandwich
Räksmörgås

4 slices white sandwich bread
margarine or butter
4 lettuce leaves
4 hard-boiled eggs, sliced
400 g (14 oz.) fresh cooked shrimps

Dressing
1 dl mayonnaise
2 tablespoons chili-sauce
salt, pepper

Trim the crust. Spread the bread and cover it with lettuce and sliced eggs. Peel the shrimps and put on top. Beat together the ingredients for the dressing and pour over the shrimps. If desired, garnish with a few shrimps on top, dill sprigs and a piece of lemon.

Lapp Sandwich
Lappsmörgås

6 to 8 eggs
½ dl (¼ cup) water
¼ teaspoon salt
white pepper
2 to 3 tablespoons
margarine or butter

4 slices soft tunnbröd or 4 slices white
   sandwich bread
margarine or butter
150 g (about 5 oz.) sliced smoked reindeer meat
parsley

Beat the eggs lightly with a fork. If desired, add the water for softer eggs. Season with salt and a pinch of freshly ground white pepper. In a heavy-bottomed saucepan, melt the fat. Add the egg-batter and cook over medium-low heat, stirring continually. When beginning to set, remove from heat and let cool.

Spread the bread with margarine or butter. Cover with the meat and put a generous spoonful of the cold scrambled eggs on top. If possible, make a cone. Garnish with parsley.

Variation: Substitute dried beef for the reindeer meat.

Herring Sandwich
Sillsmörgås

4 slices dark rye bread
margarine or butter
lettuce
3 small boiled potatoes
1 red onion, sliced
1 can herring tidbits in tomato sauce
dill or chives

Spread the bread with margarine or butter. Put a small lettuce leaf on each sandwich and cover with sliced potatoes. Arrange the herring on top. Garnish with chopped dill, chives and red onion rings.

Giant Gourmet Sandwich
Delikatesslandgång

1 slice white sandwich bread, cut lengthwise
margarine or butter

  I. 1 to 2 tablespoons whipped cream
     dill or parsley
     1 slice smoked salmon

 II. 1 small, curved, light green lettuce
     leaf
     1 tablespoon mayonnaise
     paprika
     6 to 8 peeled shrimps
     1 lemon wedge

III. 2 tablespoons liver pâté or mush-
     room paste
     2 to 3 large slices cooked chicken
     sliced pimento or tomato wedges
     parsley sprig

IV. 1 slice Swiss cheese
     1 small triangle of Gorgonzola
     cheese
     lettuce leaves or 2 to 3 radishes or
     olives

Trim the crust and spread the bread with margarine or butter. Mark the bread in four sections.

I. Mix the whipped cream with enough chopped dill or parsley to color it a pale green. Spoon the cream over the first section. Roll up the salmon and put on top. Garnish with a nice sprig of dill.

II. Cover the second section with lettuce. Season the mayonnaise with paprika and put on top. Garnish with the shrimps and lemon wedge.

III. Spread the third part with liver pâté or mushroom paste. Cover with sliced chicken. Garnish with pimento or thin tomato wedges and a small parsley sprig.

IV. Cover the fourth and last section with the two kinds of cheese. Garnish with lettuce leaves, radishes or olives.

Salads

All of the salads presented here may be served as part of a smörgåsbord. The herring salad and west coast salad both make an excellent first course or late supper dish; the other salads may be served as accompaniments for a fish or meat dish.

Herring Salad
Sillsallad

2 to 4 fillets of salt herring
   or 1 can soaked fillets of salt herring
2 to 3 cold cooked potatoes
2 pickled beets
1 large apple
1 pickled cucumber
100 to 150 g (3½ to 5 oz.) cooked ham
1 to 2 tablespoons liquid from pickled
   beets
white pepper
1 to 1½ dl (½ to ¾ cup) whipping cream
1 hard-boiled egg
finely chopped parsley

Soak the fillets in lots of cold water for 6 to
8 hours, or follow the directions on the
package. Cut the potatoes, beets, apple,
cucumber, ham and herring in small
cubes. Mix it all and combine with liquid
from pickled beets and a little pepper.

    Whip the cream and fold into the salad.
Transfer to a serving bowl and garnish
with strips of finely chopped egg white,
egg yolk and parsley. Or pack the salad in
a bowl, then unmold and garnish.

Mushroom Salad
Champinjonsallad

200 g (7 oz.) raw mushrooms

Dressing
1½ tablespoons red wine vinegar
4 tablespoons oil
salt, white pepper
garlic salt or garlic powder

Trim and cut the mushrooms in thin
slices. Mix the ingredients for the dressing
and pour over the mushrooms. Leave to
marinate for at least 1 hour; stir the salad
now and then.

Tomato Salad
Tomatsallad

4 to 5 large tomatoes
1 medium onion
finely chopped parsley

Dressing
1 tablespoon red wine vinegar
½ teaspoon salt
white pepper
2 teaspoons chervil
4 tablespoons oil

Cut the tomatoes with a sharp knife in very
thin slices; arrange these in rows on a
platter, one slice overlapping the other. Or
dip the tomatoes in boiling water and peel
before cutting in half, then remove the
seeds. Chop the onion finely and sprinkle
over the tomatoes.

    Beat together the ingredients for the
dressing and pour over the salad. Chill.
Sprinkle with chopped parsley imme-
diately before serving.

Variation: Add 100 to 150 g (3½ to 5 oz.)
sliced raw mushrooms to the salad. Or add
sliced olives.

*West coast salad can be
served as a first course, a
lunch or a late supper dish.*

50

West Coast Salad
Västkustsallad

200 g (7 oz.) fresh cooked shrimps
1 fresh cooked lobster or 6 to 8 cooked
    sea-crayfish or equivalent amount
    canned shellfish
100 g (3½ oz.) raw mushrooms
1 head lettuce
2 tomatoes
1 small can asparagus
and/or
1 small pkg frozen peas

Dressing
2 tablespoons red wine vinegar
salt, white pepper
6 tablespoons oil

Peel the shrimps. Pick the meat from the
lobster or sea-crayfish; cut in small pieces.
Slice the mushrooms and shred the lettuce. Cut the tomatoes in thin wedges.
Mix all the ingredients.
    Shake together the ingredients for the
dressing, blend with the salad. Chill before
serving.
    Serve the salad with toast as a first
course or as a luncheon or supper dish.

White Cabbage and
Lingonberry Salad
Vitkålssallad med lingon

1 wedge white cabbage (200 g or 7 oz.)
1 dl (½ cup) lingonberry preserve

Shred the cabbage finely. Mix with the
lingonberry preserve and chill before
serving.

Cucumber Salad
Inlagd gurka

1 medium cucumber (about 500 g
    or 1 lb.)

Dressing
¾ dl (½ cup) Swedish spirit vinegar
2½ dl (1¼ cups) water
¾ dl (½ cup) sugar
finely chopped parsley

Cut the cucumber in thin slices.
    Mix the vinegar, water and sugar; set
aside for a few minutes, stirring now and
then till the sugar is dissolved. Pour the
dressing over the cucumber and add a
generous sprinkling of finely chopped
parsley. Chill for about 2 hours before
serving.

Red Cabbage Salad
Rödkålssallad

1 wedge red cabbage (200 g or 7 oz.)
1 dl (½ cup) apple sauce (unsweetened or
    lightly sweetened)
2 to 3 teaspoons grated horseradish

Shred the cabbage finely. Mix the apple
sauce and grated horseradish; blend with
the cabbage. Serve the salad well chilled.

Beet Salad
Rödbetssallad

2 to 3 pickled beets
2 cold cooked potatoes
1 small apple, peeled
2 tablespoons thinly sliced leek

Dressing
1½ to 2 dl (¾ to 1 cup) sour cream
2 tablespoons finely chopped pickled
    cucumber
prepared Swedish mustard,
salt, white pepper

Dice the beets, potatoes and apple; mix
with the leek. Flavor the cream with chopped pickled cucumber, mustard and
spices. Blend the salad with the dressing.
Chill before serving. If desired, garnish
with thin rings of leek.

Soups

Compared with other European nations, Swedes cannot be called a soup-loving people. Still, a common lunch is a bowl of soup with a crispbread sandwich and cheese. At a formal dinner, soup is often the first course. And at least once a week, a rich hearty soup is served for supper in Swedish homes.

Yellow pea soup and pancakes is the traditional Thursday supper since centuries back. During Catholic times, the heavy fare probably served to fortify the people before Friday which was fastingday. Sweden converted to the Lutheran Church in the sixteenth century but the pea soup tradition is still cherished.

Yellow pea soup with mustard and pork shank, on festive occasions served with hot Swedish arrack punch.

Cabbage Soup
Brynt vitkålssoppa

¼ **to ½ head white cabbage (about 500 g
or 1 lb.)**
2 tablespoons margarine or butter
1¼ liter (5 cups) beef bouillon (cube)
salt, white pepper

Trim the cabbage and shred or cut it in
small even pieces. Discard the coarser
parts. Melt the margarine or butter in a
kettle, add the cabbage. Cook, stirring,
over medium heat until the cabbage is
nicely browned. Add the bouillon. Cover
and let the soup simmer until the cabbage
is tender: fresh summer cabbage 15 to 30
minutes, winter cabbage up to 1½ hours.

Season with salt and pepper. Serve the
soup with meat quenelles or pork sausage.
The quenelles and the sausage may be
cooked in the soup.

Variation: The cabbage may be cooked
without browning; the soup will then be
lighter and have a milder taste. Add, if you
like, sliced carrots and leek to this soup.

Meat Quenelles
Frikadeller

1 tablespoon fine dry bread crumbs
1 dl milk
200 g ground veal
½ teaspoon salt
allspice
1 egg

Mix bread crumbs with milk. Set aside for
5 minutes. Work together veal, salt, allspice and egg. Gradually add the bread
crumbs. Blend well.

Shape into balls with two teaspoons and
cook in the boiling soup for a few minutes.

Nettle Soup
Nässelsoppa

2 liter (8 cups) young tender nettles
1¼ liter (5 cups) beef bouillon (cube)
2 to 3 tablespoons flour
2 tablespoons margarine or butter
salt, white pepper
1 teaspoon chervil
finely chopped chives

Garnish
2 hardboiled eggs or 4 poached eggs

Rinse the nettles well, let cook in the
bouillon till tender. Strain and chop or
grind the nettles finely. Return the nettles
and cooking liquid to the kettle; bring to a
boil.

Stir together the flour and margarine or
butter, add to the soup. Let cook for a few
minutes. Season the soup to taste with salt,
pepper, pounded chervil and chives. Serve
with hardboiled eggs cut in half or
poached eggs.

Spinach soup and *kale soup* may be prepared in the same way. Frozen spinach or
kale may be substituted for fresh.

Yellow Pea Soup
Gul ärtsoppa

4 dl (1¾ cups) dried yellow peas
1½ liter (6½ cups) water
1 tablespoon salt
300 to 400 g (10½ to 14 oz.) lightly salted
  side pork or 1 small pork shank
water
1 pinch ginger, thyme or marjoram

Rinse the peas and let soak in cold water with salt for 10 to 12 hours. Drain. Add 1 liter water. Season with salt. Cover and cook rapidly for a few minutes. Skim off the shells floating on the surface. Add the whole piece of pork. Or cut the pork in cubes and add when the peas have cooked for 30 minutes.

Let the soup simmer for 1 to 1½ hours or till peas and pork are tender. Add more water to the soup if too thick. Season with salt, ginger, thyme or marjoram. Remove the pork, cut in slices and serve apart or cut in cubes and return to the soup.

Vegetable Soup
Grönsakssoppa

1 small cauliflower
2 dl (1 cup) fresh peas or 1 small pkg
  frozen peas
4 tender carrots
1 leek
8 dl (3½ cups) water
salt
4 to 5 dl (1¾ to 2 cups) milk
2 tablespoons flour
2 tablespoons margarine or butter
salt, white pepper
2 tablespoons finely chopped parsley

Rinse and trim the vegetables. Divide the cauliflower into florets and cut the carrots in pieces. Cut the leek in thin slices. Let the vegetables cook in the water with salt until almost tender. Add the milk.

Stir together the flour and margarine or butter, add to the soup and cook for a few minutes. Season the soup to taste. Sprinkle with finely chopped parsley.

Fish Soup
Fisksoppa

1 to 2 carrots
1 leek
1 tablespoon margarine or butter
1½ tablespoons flour
1 liter fish bouillon (cube)
1 bay leaf
500 g fresh or frozen fillets of fish
    or 1 can fishballs in bouillon
400 g frozen peas and carrots
salt, white pepper
dill, parsley

Trim and slice the carrots and leek. In a
saucepan, heat the margarine or butter.
Add the vegetables and cook for a few
minutes. Sprinkle with flour. Add the fish
bouillon or water and fish bouillon cube
and bay leaf.

Let the soup simmer covered till the
vegetables are almost tender. Then add the
fish fillets or fishballs in slices and let the
soup simmer for a few minutes. Add the
frozen vegetables. Taste and adjust the
seasoning.

Sprinkle the soup with chopped dill or
parsley.

Beef and Vegetable Soup
Köttsoppa

200—300 g boneless beef (rib, rump, bris-
    ket or bottom round) or 500 g beef with
    bones
1 tablespoon margarine or butter
1½ liter water
2 carrots
1 parsnip
1 piece celeriac (celery root)
2 leeks
4 potatoes
1½—2 teaspoons salt
8 whole white pepper
chopped parsley

Cut the meat in small cubes. Heat the
margarine or butter in a saucepan. When
the foam subsides, add the meat and
brown it on all sides. Add 5 dl of water and
meatbones. Cover and simmer till almost
tender, about 45 minutes.

Rinse, trim and cut the vegetables and
potatoes in pieces. Add them and the rest
of the water, salt and peppercorns. Cover
and simmer till tender about 20 minutes.

Serve with chopped parsley.

Vegetable Dishes

S wedish cooking can be divided into two periods, before and after the potato. For two centuries this tuber has been an all-important staple in the diet of the Swedish people.

Today a wide variety of vegetables such as cabbage, carrots, corn, peas, leek, broccoli, brussels sprouts and spinach are popular, too, but potatoes are still served almost daily in many Swedish homes. Sweden has a number of good potato dishes but usually potatoes are served boiled in their jackets.

Boiled Potatoes Swedish Style

Nothing tastes better than Swedish dill potatoes. Scrub small new potatoes clean and drop into boiling salted water together with sprigs of fresh dill. Cook, covered, over moderate heat till tender or about 15 minutes. Test with a toothpick. Drain off the water and let the steam disappear. Serve at once.

To cook the larger winter potatoes, select potatoes of the same size and scrub them clean. If desired, peel the potatoes before putting them in a saucepan. Add water to cover and 2 tablespoons salt for each kg potatoes. Bring to a boil, cover and turn down the heat. Let simmer till tender or about 20 minutes. Drain well and let the steam disappear. Serve at once.

Potatoes in White Sauce
Råstuvad potatis

¾ kg (about 1 lb. 10 oz.) potatoes
4 dl (1¾ cups) milk
1 tablespoon margarine or butter
salt, white pepper
finely chopped parsley

Wash and peel the potatoes, cut in slices or cubes. In a saucepan, bring the milk and margarine or butter to a boil. Add the potatoes and cook, covered, till tender. Season to taste with salt and pepper. Sprinkle with chopped parsley.

Serve with fried meat, fish or sausage.

Hasselback Potatoes
Hasselbackspotatis

12 small oblong potatoes
3 tablespoons margarine or butter
salt
3 tablespoons grated cheese

Wash and peel the potatoes. Cut in thin slices without cutting quite through; the potato should remain whole at the bottom. If large potatoes are used, cut in half lengthwise and place cut side down before slicing.

Put the potatoes sliced side up in a well buttered baking dish. Sprinkle with salt and dot with margarine or butter. Bake in a 225°C oven for 20 minutes. Sprinkle with cheese and bake for another 20 minutes.

Potato Pancakes
Rårakor

1 kg (2 lb. 3 oz.) potatoes
1½ teaspoons salt
½ dl (¼ cup) water
50 to 75 g (about 2 to 2½ oz.) margarine,
    butter or bacon fat

Peel and grate the potatoes. Mix with salt and water. Drop the batter in large tablespoonfuls into a skillet with hot fat. Cook the pancakes over medium-high heat till crisp and brown on both sides.

If possible, serve the pancakes directly from the pan with fried pork and lingonberry preserve.

Carrots in White Sauce
Stuvade morötter

**500 to 600 g (1 lb. 1 oz. to 1 lb. 5 oz.)
carrots
water, salt**

Sauce
**1 to 1½ tablespoons margarine or butter
3 tablespoons flour
3 to 4 dl (1½ to 2 cups) milk mixed with
liquid from cooking the carrots
salt, white pepper
3 to 4 tablespoons finely chopped parsley**

Peel and cut the carrots in cubes or slices.
Cook in lightly salted water till tender.
Drain well.

In a saucepan, melt the margarine or
butter. Stir in the flour. Add the milk and
bring to a boil beating the sauce until
smooth. Let cook for a few minutes. Season to taste with salt and pepper. Fold in
the cooked carrots and parsley.

Instead of carrots, any kind of vegetables, e.g. peas, beans or white cabbage,
may be used. Or mix the sauce with
cooked potatoes cut in cubes.

Brown Beans
Bruna bönor

**4 dl dried brown beans (about 350 g
or 12 oz.)
1¼ liter (5 cups) water
1 teaspoon salt
2 to 3 tablespoons white vinegar or red
wine vinegar
2 to 3 tablespoons syrup**

Rinse the beans and soak in the water for
10 to 12 hours. Bring to a boil in the same
water the beans have been soaked in, add
salt and cook, covered, for 2 to 2½ hours.
Season to taste with vinegar and syrup.

When a pressure cooker is used, reduce
the water to 1 liter and cook for 25 to 30
minutes.

Red Cabbage
Rödkål

**¾ kg (about 1 lb. 10 oz.) red cabbage
2 to 3 tablespoons margarine or butter
¼ to ½ dl (¼ cup) syrup
1 small yellow onion
2 to 3 tablespoons red wine vinegar
1 to 2 apples, peeled and cut in wedges
1 tablespoon salt
white pepper or allspice**

Shred the cabbage finely. Melt the margarine or butter in a heavy saucepan, add
the cabbage and syrup. Cook over medium
heat for about 15 minutes, stirring occasionally.

Grate the onion and add together with
the vinegar and apples. Cook, covered,
over low heat for about 1½ hours or till the
cabbage is tender. Stir now and then so
that the cabbage does not burn. Season to
taste with salt and pepper or allspice.

Pressure cooker may be used for this
dish; cook for about 15 minutes.

Baked Mushroom Omelette with Sausages
Svamplåda med korv

1 can (about 200 g or 7 oz) mixed mushrooms, drained
2 tablespoons margarine or butter
salt, white pepper

Omelette
4 teaspoons flour
4 dl (1¾ cups) milk
4 beaten eggs
salt, pepper

6 to 9 Swedish prince sausages or small
  frankfurters
margarine or butter

Chop the mushrooms and sauté in the
margarine or butter. Season lightly with
salt and pepper. Transfer the mushrooms
to a buttered baking dish.

To make the omelette, stir the flour
with part of the milk to a smooth batter.
Bring the remaining milk to a boil, stir in
the flour mixture. Cook for 3 minutes and
then let cool. Add the eggs and mix well.
Season with salt and pepper, pour the
batter over the mushrooms. Bake for
about 30 minutes in a 175 to 200° oven.

Sauté the sausages in a little hot margarine or butter and arrange on top of the
omelette in the shape of a "star". Serve
with tomato sauce.

Herring and Fish

S weden, a country of close to 100,000 lakes, innumerable rivers and a long coastal line, has always made good use of its rich supply of fish and shellfish. Among the different kinds of fish available, herring has of old a special position, so that Swedes always differentiate between *sill* and *fisk* or herring and fish. Various preparations with salt and fresh herring are a must on the smörgåsbord.

A close relative to the herring is *strömming* or, as it is sometimes called, Baltic herring. This small silvery fish is a favorite food of the people along the east coast. In late summer, *surströmming*, fermented strömming, is enjoyed at special parties. *Gravlax*, salmon, cured with salt, sugar and dill, and *lutfisk*, ling cured with lye, are two other all-Swedish delicacies.

Salt Herring
Spicken sill

4 to 6 fillets of salt herring
2 to 3 tablespoons finely chopped chives
1 tablespoon finely chopped onion

Soak the herring in lots of cold water for 1 to 2 hours. Drain and cut in 2 cm thick slices. Place on serving platter and sprinkle with chopped chives and onion.

Serve with hot boiled potatoes and ice-cold sour cream. Or serve with potatoes in white sauce flavored with onion and dill.

Glassblower's Herring
Glasmästarsill

2 to 3 whole salt herrings

Dressing
1½ to 2 dl (1 to 1¾ cups) sugar
1 dl (½ cup) Swedish spirit vinegar
2 dl (about 1 cup) water
5 whole allspice
1 bay leaf
1 carrot, sliced
½ leek, sliced
1 red onion, sliced
1 thin slice of horseradish

Clean the herring and soak in lots of cold water for 12 hours. Scrape the herring and rinse well. Cut across in 1½ to 2 cm thick slices.

Stir together the sugar, vinegar and water. Bring to a boil together with the allspice and bay leaf; let cool. Put the herring and vegetables in layers in a glas jar. Pour in the dressing which should cover the herring completely. Refrigerate for at least 4–6 days before serving.

Rollmops
Rollmops

4 to 6 fillets of salt herring or 1 can
soaked fillets of salt herring

Filling
½ teaspoon crushed black peppercorns
½ teaspoon crushed white peppercorns
1 red onion, finely chopped
½ dl (¼ cup) finely chopped dill

Dressing
1 dl (½ cup) Swedish spirit vinegar
1½ dl (¾ cup) water
1½ dl (¾ cup) sugar
½ dl (¼ cup) tomato ketchup or chili
sauce

Soak the herring in lots of cold water for 10 to 12 hours, or follow the directions on the package. Drain. Stir together the ingredients for the filling and spread on top of the fillets. Roll up each fillet starting from the head end; secure the rolls with toothpicks. Place the rolls in a jar or bowl.

Bring the vinegar, water and sugar to a boil. Let cool and flavor the dressing with tomato ketchup or chili sauce. Cover the rolls with the dressing and refrigerate for at least 24 hours before serving.

To serve, cut each roll in thin slices and garnish with red onion rings and dill sprigs.

Pickled Herring
Inlagd sill

4 to 6 fillets of salt herring or 1 can soaked fillets of salt herring

Dressing
1½ dl (¾ cup) sugar
1 dl (½ cup) Swedish spirit vinegar
2 dl (about 1 cup) water
5 coarsely crushed allspice
1 bay leaf
1 to 2 red onions, sliced
dill sprigs

Soak the herring in lots of cold water for 10 to 12 hours, or follow the directions on the package. Drain. Stir together the sugar, vinegar and water. Add the allspice, bay leaf and onion. Pour the dressing over the herring and refrigerate for at least 24 hours. Then cut the herring in 1 cm thick slices, cover with dressing and garnish with red onion rings and dill sprigs.

Variation: Instead of allspice, add 1 teaspoon whole cloves and 5 crushed white peppercorns to the dressing. Bring to a boil, let cool and pour over the herring saving about ½ dl (¼ cup). Refrigerate for at least 12 hours. Slice the herring and place in serving dish. Add the remaining dressing and garnish with red onion rings, cloves and dill.

Pickled Stromming
Gravad strömming

1 kg (2 lb. 3 oz.) whole stromming or 600 g (1 lb. 5 oz.) fillets of stromming
water
2 tablespoons salt
½ dl (¼ cup) Swedish spirit vinegar for each liter water

Dressing
½ dl (¼ cup) prepared Swedish mustard
3 tablespoons sugar
1 teaspoon salt
1 teaspoon coarsely crushed white peppercorns
1½ dl (¾ cup) oil
1 tablespoon spirit vinegar
½ to 1 dl (¼ to ½ cup) finely chopped dill

Clean and fillet the fish. Remove the skin. (If this is difficult to do, wait until the fish has soaked in the vinegar for a while.) Put the fillets in water mixed with salt and vinegar for 1 to 2 hours. Drain.

Stir together the mustard, sugar, salt and pepper for the dressing. Gradually add the oil, then the vinegar and dill.

Put the fish and dressing in layers in a deep serving dish. Refrigerate for at least 24 hours.

Serve cold with hot boiled potatoes. The fish will keep for 1 week in refrigerator.

*Glassblower's herring,
herring salad and pickled
herring.*

66

Tarragon Stromming
Dragonströmming

¾ kg (1 lb. 10 oz) whole stromming
4 dl (1¾ cups) water
3 tablespoons Swedish spirit vinegar
1½ teaspoons salt

Dressing
1 dl (½ cup) or 100 g (3½ oz.) mayonnaise
1 dl (½ cup) sour cream or whipping
   cream
½ to 1 crushed garlic clove
salt, white pepper
1 teaspoon dried tarragon
2 to 3 tablespoons finely chopped parsley

Clean and fillet the stromming. Remove
the skin. Stir together the water, vinegar
and salt; pour over the fish and refrigerate
for 24 hours. Drain well.

Stir the mayonnaise with sour cream or
whipped cream. Season to taste with
garlic, salt, pepper, tarragon and parsley.
Pour the dressing over the fish and chill
for about 1 hour.

Serve with toast and cool beer.

Crayfish Stromming
Kräftströmming

¾ kg (1 lb. 10 oz.) whole stromming or
   1 to 2 packages frozen fillets of stromming
2 to 3 teaspoons salt
1 can (about 250 g or 8 oz tomato juice

2 tablespoons dill seed or 4 to 5 tablespoons finely chopped dill

Clean the fish and remove the back bone;
rinse well. Thaw the frozen fish. Sprinkle
with salt and roll up each fillet, skinside
in. Put the rolls close to each other in a
wide shallow casserole. Pour over the
tomato juice blended with dill or dillseeds.
Bring to a simmer and cook, covered, over
low heat for 20 to 30 minutes. Chill well.
Sprinkle with dill and serve.

Fried Salt Herring with Onions and Cream Sauce
Stekt salt sill med lök och gräddsky

4 fillets of salt herring or 1 can soaked
   fillets of salt herring
1 dl (about ½ cup) rye flour or ½ dl (¼
   cup) fine dry bread crumbs
½ dl (¼ cup) flour
magarine or butter
2 onions, sliced
2 dl (about 1 cup) light cream

Soak the fillets for 10 to 12 hours, or
follow the directions on the package.
Drain well. Dip the herring in rye flour or
bread crumbs mixed with flour. Fry in hot
margarine or butter till browned on both
sides, transfer to serving platter.

Then fry the sliced onions till a golden
brown and spread on top of the herring.

Add the cream to the skillet and bring to a boil, stirring.

Serve the herring with the hot cream sauce. Or serve the herring with white sauce made with milk and flavored with sautéed chopped onion.

Matjes Herring
Matjessill

1 can matjes herring
dill sprigs
½ dl (¼ cup) chopped chives
2 dl (about 1 cup) sour cream

Drain the herring and cut in serving pieces. Slide a spatula under the herring and transfer to an oblong serving dish so that the fillets look whole. Chill and garnish with dill sprigs, if desired.

Serve with chopped chives, sour cream and hot new dill potatoes. Sliced green pepper and sliced red or yellow onion may also be served with matjes herring.

Fried Fresh Herring with Mustard
Senapsstekt sill

1 kg (2 lb. 3 oz.) fresh herring
2 egg yolks
2 tablespoons prepared Swedish mustard
2 tablespoons whipping cream
1 dl (½ cup) fine dry bread crumbs
margarine or butter

Clean and fillet the herring. Rinse well, drain and sprinkle with salt. Stir together the egg yolks, mustard and cream. Dip the herring into the batter, then into the bread crumbs.

Heat a skillet with margarine or butter. When the foam subsides, add the herring and cook over medium heat till golden brown on both sides.

Serve hot or cold with potatoes and creamed spinach.

Herring Baked in Foil
Sill i kapprock

4 to 8 fillets of salt herring or 1 can soaked fillets of salt herring
50 to 75 g (about 2 to 2¼ oz.) margarine or butter
2 hard-boiled eggs, chopped
2 to 3 tablespoons finely chopped dill

Soak the herring in lots of cold water for 10 to 12 hours, or follow the directions on the package.

Put each fillet on a piece of aluminum foil or grease-proof paper. Dot with margarine or butter and sprinkle each fillet with chopped egg and dill. Fold the paper or foil around the herring and put the parcels in a baking dish in a 200°C oven. Bake for about 10 minutes. Instead of dill, chopped onion may be used.

Anchovy Eye
Solöga

8 Swedish anchovy fillets, chopped
2 tablespoons chopped onion
2 tablespoons capers
2 tablespoons chives
3 tablespoons diced pickled beets
2 to 4 raw egg yolks

Arrange anchovy fillets, onion, capers, chives and beets in circles on one large or 4 serving plates and place egg yolks in center.

Stir the ingredients until well blended just before eating.

Serve with toast and butter.

Jansson's Temptation
Janssons frestelse

6 to 8 potatoes
2 onions
2 to 3 tablespoons margarine or butter
1 to 2 cans anchovy fillets
2½ to 3 dl (1¼ to 1½ cups) light cream

Peel the potatoes, cut in thin sticks. Slice the onions. Sauté the onion lightly in some of the margarine or butter. Drain the anchovies and cut in pieces.

Put the potatoes, onion and anchovies in layers in buttered baking dish. The first and last layer should be potatoes. Dot with margarine or butter on top. Pour in a little of the liquid from the anchovies and half of the cream.

Anchovy eye.

Bake in a 200°C oven for about 20 minutes. Pour in the remaining cream and bake for another 30 minutes or till the potatoes are tender.

Serve as a first course or supper dish.

Herring au Gratin with Potatoes
Sillgratäng med potatis

4 to 6 fillets of salt herring or 1 can
    soaked fillets of salt herring
2 large onions, sliced
3 tablespoons margarine or butter
500 g (about 1 lb.) potatoes, peeled and
    sliced
1 leek, sliced
2 tablespoons fine dry bread crumbs
2 dl (about 1 cup) light cream
1 dl (½ cup) milk
finely chopped dill

Soak the herring in lots of cold water for 12 hours, or follow the directions on the package. Sauté the onion in some of the margarine or butter.

Place the potatoes, leek, herring and onion in rows in a buttered baking dish. Sprinkle with bread crumbs and dot with margarine or butter. Bake in a 200°C to 225°C oven for 20 minutes. Add the cream and milk. Bake for another 25 to 30 minutes. Sprinkle with chopped dill and serve hot.

Instead of raw potatoes, boiled potatoes may be used; then reduce the liquid and allow 20 minutes total baking time.

Fried Stromming
Strömmingsflundror

¾ to 1 kg (1 lb. 10 oz. to 2 lb. 3 oz.) whole
  stromming or 1 pkg frozen fillets of
  stromming
flour, fine dry bread crumbs
salt, white pepper
margarine, butter or oil

Filling
2 tablespoons margarine or butter
50 g (about 2 oz.) finely chopped parsley
  or 3 to 4 tablespoons grated horseradish

Clean the fish and remove the backbone.
Thaw the frozen fish.

Stir the margarine or butter with chopped parsley or grated horseradish. Put two
fillets together, skinside out, with a little
filling between. Dip both sides in flour
mixed with bread crumbs, salt and pepper.

Heat a skillet with margarine, butter or
oil. When the foam subsides, add the fish
and fry both sides till a golden brown.

Serve at once with mashed or boiled
potatoes and creamed vegetables.

Stromming Casserole
Strömmingslåda

1 kg (2 lb. 3 oz.) whole stromming
1 tablespoon salt
1 teaspoon 4-spices
1 leek, sliced

5 tablespoons grated cheese
1 dl (½ cup) light cream
2 tablespoons margarine or butter
2 tomatoes, sliced
finely chopped parsley

Clean the fish and remove the backbone.
Rinse and drain. Sprinkle with salt and
fold each fish so that it looks whole. Place
the fish, belly down, in a buttered baking
dish. Sprinkle with the spices, then the
sliced leek and, finally, the cheese. Pour in
the cream and dot with margarine or butter.

Add the sliced tomatoes either before or
after baking. Bake in a 200°C oven for
about 30 minutes.

Serve hot; sprinkle with chopped
parsley before serving.

Buckling in Mustard Marinade
Senapsmarinerad böckling

3 to 4 bucklings (smoked stromming) or 1
  large smoked herring

Marinade
2 to 3 tablespoons oil
1 tablespoon red wine vinegar
1 to 2 tablespoons prepared mustard
white pepper

Garnish
1 tart apple, diced
1 onion, diced
1 pickled beet, diced

2 tablespoons finely chopped dill
lemon juice

Clean and fillet the fish. Remove as many small bones as possible. Put the fillets on a serving platter.

Beat together the ingredients for the marinade, season it to taste and pour over the fish.

Garnish with rows of diced apple, onion, beet and dill. Press a little lemon juice over the apple to prevent discoloring.

Broiled Perch
Halstrad abborre

1 to 1¼ kg (2 lb. 3 oz. to 2 lb. 11½ oz.)
perch
oil

Broil the perch whole or in fillets, as desired. When broiled whole, the fish need not be scaled, just cleaned. Brush with oil and broil for 8 to 10 minutes over a grill, in a rack over open fire or in hot ungreased cast iron skillet.

Remove the skin and serve with salt and butter flavored with lemon juice.

Whitefish, whiting, herring and *trout* may be prepared in the same way.

Summer Casserole
Sommargryta

6 to 8 perch or whiting (about 1½ kg or
2 lb. 5 oz.)
1 tablespoon salt
½ to 1 dl (¼ to ½ cup) finely chopped dill
and chives
2 tablespoons flour
2 to 3 tablespoons margarine or butter
juice of ½ to 1 lemon
water
4 tomatoes, cut in wedges

Clean and fillet the fish. Rinse quickly and sprinkle with salt. Put the fish and chopped herbs in layers in a casserole that can be brought to the table.

Stir together the flour and margarine or butter to a smooth paste; dot over the fish. Add the lemon juice and enough water to reach halfway up the fish.

Let the fish simmer, covered, for a few minutes, then add the tomato wedges. Let simmer for a few minutes more.

Serve hot with boiled potatoes and a tossed sallad.

Frozen *cod, haddock* and other fish may be prepared in the same way. Thaw the fish slightly and cut in slices.

Chimney Sweepers
Sotare

¾ to 1 kg (1 lb. 10 oz. to 2 lb. 3 oz.) whole
   stromming
1 tablespoon salt
oil

Salt water
1 liter (4 cups) water
3 tablespoons salt

Green cream
1 to 1½ dl (½ to ¾ cup) light cream
finely chopped chives
parsley and dill
salt, white pepper

Clean the fish but do not remove the
backbone, only the head, tail and intestines. Rinse well and rub with salt. Brush
with oil and broil the fish for 3 to 4
minutes in a hot cast iron skillet or inside a
rack over open fire.

   Immerse the fish in the salt water for a
second and serve at once with green cream
and potatoes boiled in their jackets. Flavor
the cream with finely chopped herbs, salt
and pepper to taste.

*Chimney sweepers broiled
over open fire.*

Fried Plaice with Capers and Beets
Stekt rödspättefilé med kapris och rödbeta

500 g (about 1 lb.) fresh or 1 pkg frozen
   fillets of plaice
1 egg white, lightly beaten
2 tablespoons flour
2 tablespoons fine dry bread crumbs
½ to ¾ tablespoon salt
75 g (2¼ oz.) margarine or butter

Garnish
2 tablespoons capers
3 tablespoons finely chopped pickled
   beets
1 tablespoon finely chopped parsley

Thaw frozen fish. Cut obliquely in 2 cm
thick slices. Dip the fish in the beaten egg
white, then in the flour mixed with bread
crumbs and salt.

   Heat a skillet with part of the margarine
or butter. When the foam subsides, add
the fish and fry till a golden brown. Remove to heated serving platter. Brown the
remaining margarine or butter; stir in the
capers, beets and parsley. Heat and pour
over the fish.

   Serve with boiled potatoes.

Most kinds of fish, e.g. *cod, haddock,
mackerel* and *herring*, may be prepared in
the same way.

Baked Fish with Mushroom Sauce
Fiskgratäng med champinjoner

¾ to 1 kg (1½ to 2 lb.) fillets of halibut,
  cod, pike, perch or sole
margarine or butter
1 dl (½ cup) fish bouillon (cube)
1 dl dry white wine
1 tablespoon lemon juice
2 teaspoons salt

Mushroom Sauce
2 cans (à 100 g size) mushrooms
50 g margarine or butter
3 tablespoons all-purpose flour
2½ dl fish bouillon
1 dl light cream
salt
1 spice spoon ground nutmeg

1½ dl (¾ cup) grated cheese

Arrange fish fillets side by side in a close-fitting buttered baking dish. Pour over fish bouillon, wine and lemon juice. Sprinkle with salt, cover with aluminum foil and bake in 200°C oven for 10 to 20 minutes. Holding fish in place with a spatula, drain juices into measuring cup. Cover and keep the fish warm.

Cook the thinly sliced mushrooms in margarine or butter until mushrooms are limp and juices have evaporated. Blend in flour. Stir and blend in fish liquid and cream. Bring to boil and cook 1 to 2 minutes until thickened. Add salt and nutmeg to taste.

Spoon sauce evenly over poached fish and cover completely. Sprinkle grated cheese over and bake the fish in 200°C oven for 10 to 15 minutes, until sauce is bubbling and cheese has melted.

Serve with boiled potatoes.

Pickled Salmon
Inkokt lax

1 kg (2 lb. 3 oz.) fresh salmon
¾ tablespoon salt
1 bay leaf
4 to 5 white peppercorns
a few dill sprigs
2 slices onion
½ liter (2 cups) warm water
½ to 1 dl (¼ to ½ cup) Swedish table
  vinegar

Clean and rinse the fish, cut in pieces 3 to 4 cm thick. Put the fish in a low, wide saucepan or fish kettle. Add the spices, dill and onion. Pour in the water mixed with vinegar. Let simmer for 8 to 10 minutes. Transfer the fish to a serving dish and pour the hot stock over. Let cool.

Serve with cold mayonnaise sauce.

Eel, mackerel, lumpfish and *herring* may be prepared in the same way.

Mayonnaise Sauce
Majonnässås

2 dl mayonnaise
2 dl sour cream
salt, white pepper

Stir together the mayonnaise and cream. Season to taste with salt and pepper. Flavor the sauce with any of following:

- 2 tablespoons chopped, cooked spinach 1 dl chopped dill, chives, tarragon and parsley
- 1 dl chopped pickled vegetables
- ½ dl chili sauce or tomato ketchup

Gravlax

1 to 1¼ kg (2 lb. 3 oz. to 2 lb. 12 oz.) fresh or frozen salmon, center cut
¾ dl (½ cup) salt
¾ dl (½ cup) sugar
20 coarsely crushed white peppercorns
50 g (about 2 oz.) chopped dill

Half-thaw the frozen salmon. Remove the two fillets from the backbone and remove all small bones. Do not remove the skin. Wipe fillets with kitchen paper.

Mix salt and sugar with crushed peppercorns. Sprinkle some of the spice mixture in the bottom of a deep dish and lay chopped dill on top. Place one fillet on the spice and dill, skin side down. Sprinkle over half of remaining spice mixture and plenty of dill. Place second salmon fillet on top, with skin side up. Sprinkle over remainder of spice mixture and dill.

Cover dish with plastic foil. Place in refrigerator for 48 hours, turning salmon over a couple of times when juices start to collect.

To serve, scrape off spices and slice thinly at an angle as for smoked salmon, or cut into fairly thick pieces, removing skin. Garnish with fresh dill and lemon wedges. Serve with "Gravlax sauce" and toast or boiled new potatoes.

(May be frozen after pouring off juices.)

Gravlax Sauce

2 to 3 tablespoons prepared Swedish mustard
1 to 2 tablespoons sugar
1 to 2 tablespoons red wine vinegar
1 dl oil
2 to 3 tablespoons chopped dill
(salt, pepper)

Stir together mustard, sugar and vinegar. Add the oil slowly stirring all the time. Flavor with dill and serve the sauce well chilled.

Smoked Warm Salmon Trout
Rökt varm regnbågslax

1 to 1¼ kg (2 lb. 3 oz. to 2 lb. 11½ oz.)
    smoked salmon trout
lettuce
dill
radishes
lemon

Horseradish cream
1½ to 2 dl whipping cream
1 tablespoon grated horseradish
salt, white pepper
white vinegar

Wrap the fish with aluminum foil and place on a rack. Heat in a 200°C oven for 25 to 30 minutes or until thoroughly hot.

If desired, decorate the fish by making slits in the skin before putting it in the oven; after heating, pull off part of the skin. Put the fish on a heated platter and garnish with lettuce, radishes, dill and lemon wedges.

Serve with boiled new potatoes and horseradish cream.

Whip the cream and season with grated horseradish, salt, pepper and vinegar.

Salmon Pudding
Laxpudding

200 g (7 oz.) salt salmon
¾ kg (1 lb. 10 oz.) potatoes
margarine or butter
3 tablespoons chopped dill
white pepper
4 eggs
4 dl (1¾ cups) milk

Soak the fish in cold water overnight, about 12 hours. Wipe it dry and cut in pieces.

Peel and slice the potatoes. Put the potatoes and salmon in layers in a buttered baking dish. Sprinkle with dill and a little pepper between the layers. The first and last layer should be potatoes.

Beat together the eggs and milk, pour into the baking dish. Bake in a 175°C oven for about 1 hour.

Serve with melted butter.

Salmon pudding served with melted butter.

Poached Cod
Kokt torsk

**1 kg (2 lb. 3 oz.) whole cod or ¾ kg (1 lb.
10 oz.) cod, cut in thick slices**
1½ to 2 tablespoons salt
2 liter (8 cups) water
1 to 2 slices onion
2 parsley sprigs
1 lemon

Clean and rinse the fish well. Heat salt and
water in a fish kettle. Put the whole fish in
warm water, put fish cut in slices in sim-
mering water. Add the onion and parsley
sprigs. Simmer the fish slowly for 10 to 15
minutes. Transfer to serving platter and
garnish with parsley and lemon wedges.

Serve with boiled potatoes and fish
sauce. Or serve the fish with melted butter
and chopped hard-boiled egg.

Pike, pike perch, hake and other fish may
be prepared in the same way.

Fish Sauce
Fisksås

1 to 2 tablespoons margarine or butter
2 to 3 tablespoons flour
**3 to 4 dl (1½ to 1¾ cups) fish bouillon and
milk or cream**
salt, white pepper

In a saucepan, melt the margarine or butter. Stir in the flour and cook for a few
minutes. Gradually add the liquid, stirring
constantly. Use fish bouillon or milk, or
use fish bouillon mixed with milk or
cream. Let the sauce cook over medium
heat for a few minutes, stirring occasionally. Season to taste with salt and pepper.

If desired, flavor the sauce with any of
the following:

- juice of ¼ to ½ lemon
- 1 to 3 teaspoons curry powder
- 2 tablespoons finely chopped dill,
  chives, leek or parsley (fresh, frozen or
  dried)
- 1 to 2 tablespoons coarsely chopped
  capers
- 1 to 2 tablespoons salted cod roe caviar
- 100 to 150 g (3½ to 5 oz.) cooked
  cleaned shrimps
- 3 to 4 cooked cleaned sea-crayfish, cut
  in pieces
- 1 to 2 chopped hard-boiled eggs and
  parsley
- 1 to 2 tablespoons grated horseradish
- 1 to 2 tablespoons prepared Swedish
  mustard or 1 teaspoon mustard powder
- 1 to 2 tablespoons mustard seed, finely
  crushed and mixed with a little water

Ovenbaked Fillets of Whitefish
Ugnsstekt sikfilé

1 kg (2 lb. 3 oz.) whitefish
¾ tablespoon salt
1 tablespoon finely chopped onion
2 to 3 tablespoons margarine or butter

100 g (3½ oz.) **fresh mushrooms or one**
   ⅛-can mushrooms
1 dl (½ cup) **crumbed white bread**
1 to 2 tablespoons **finely chopped parsley**
water
(white vermouth)

Clean and fillet the fish. Rub with salt.
Sauté the onion in the margarine or butter.
Trim and slice or chop the mushrooms;
cook along with the onion. Pour into a
buttered baking dish and mix in the bread
crumbs and parsley. Place the fish on top.
Bake in a 200°C to 225°C oven for 10 to 15
minutes. Baste the fish often; add a little
water if necessary. For extra fine taste, add
1 to 2 tablespoons white vermouth.

Serve the fish directly from the baking
dish.

Bake whole fish in the same way; allow
20 to 25 minutes cooking time.

Carp, grayling, pike, pike perch and *whitefish* may be prepared in the same way.

Fried Mackerel with Dill Sauce
Stekt makrill med dillsky

1 kg (2 lb. 3 oz.) **mackerel**
2 tablespoons **flour**
2 tablespoons **fine dry bread crumbs**
salt, white pepper
margarine or butter
½ dl (¼ cup) **finely chopped dill**
water

Clean and fillet the fish. Rinse well and
wipe the fillets dry. Dip in the flour mixed
with bread crumbs, salt and pepper.

Heat a skillet with a little margarine or
butter. When the foam subsides, add the
fish and fry until nicely browned on both
sides. Add the dill and a little water; cook
over low heat for 10 minutes.

Serve with boiled potatoes and tomato
salad.

Ovenbaked Pike
Ugnsstekt gädda

1 kg (2 lb. 3 oz.) **pike**
lemon juice
1 egg white, **lightly beaten**
2 tablespoons **flour**
½ tablespoon **salt**
2 tablespoons **fine dry bread crumbs**
50 g (about 2 oz.) **margarine or butter**
1 small onion, **finely chopped**
2 to 3 dl (about 1 to 1½ cups) **light cream**

Clean and rinse the fish. Sprinkle with a
little fresh lemon juice. Brush with beaten
egg white and dip the fish in the flour
mixed with salt and bread crumbs. Place
the fish in a buttered baking dish and
sprinkle with chopped onion, dot with
margarine or butter. Bake in a 200°C to
225°C oven for 25 to 30 minutes. Baste the
fish now and then. When it begins to
brown, add the cream and continue bast-
ing.

Cod, whitefish, eel and other fish may be
prepared in the same way.

Ovenbaked Lutfisk
Lutfisk kokt i ugn

1½ kg (3 lb. 5 oz.) lutfisk
margarine or butter
1 tablespoon salt

Soak the fish in cold water for 1–3 hours. Drain.Place the fish, skinside down, in a buttered deep baking dish. Or, if desired, first remove the skin. (Frozen fish may be cooked in its wrapping.) Sprinkle the fish with salt and cover the dish with aluminum foil. Cook in a 200° oven for 30 to 40 minutes.

Pour off the liquid and serve the fish hot with boiled potatoes, peas, mustard sauce or lutfisk sauce, melted butter and allspice or white pepper.

Lutfisk Sauce

50 g (2 oz.) margarine or butter
3 tablespoons flour
3 to 4 dl (1½ to 1¾ cups) milk
1 teaspoon salt
white pepper

In a saucepan, melt the margarine or butter. Stir in the flour and gradually add the milk. Beat the sauce until smooth and let cook for a few minutes.

Season to taste with salt, pepper and any of the following flavors:

- coarsely crushed allspice or
- coarsely crushed blackpepper or
- 1–2 tablespoons prepared Skåne mustard

Mustard Sauce
Skånsk senapssås

1 recipe lutfisk sauce
1 tablespoon dark mustard seed
1 to 2 tablespoons water
(or 1 to 2 tablespoons prepared Skåne mustard)

Pound the mustard seed with mortar and pestle or use the special mustard ball. Mix with the water and stir into the white sauce. Or flavor the sauce with prepared mustard.

Lutfisk is often the central dish at the festive Christmas dinner. Here the ovenbaked lutfisk is served with boiled potatoes, green peas and lutfisk sauce.

Meat and Poultry

The two most common meats in Sweden are beef and pork, but veal and lamb are much used, too. The traditional Swedish Sunday dinner of veal pot roast with light cream sauce, pickled cucumber and red currant jelly is today often replaced by a fried chicken or chicken casserole, food that formerly was reserved for very special occasions only.

Reindeer meat from Lappland is available all over the country; the dark lean meat has a flavor similar to venison.

Meatballs
Köttbullar

1 dl (½ cup) fine dry bread crumbs
1 dl (½ cup) light cream
1 dl (½ cup) water
200 g (7 oz.) ground beef
200 g (7 oz.) ground lean pork
1½ teaspoons salt
½ teaspoon ground allspice
2 tablespoons grated onion
1 egg, beaten
3 tablespoons margarine or butter

Mix the bread crumbs, cream and water; set aside for 5 minutes. Work together the beef, pork, salt, allspice and onion. Gradually add the bread crumbs, then the egg. Blend well and fry a sample to test the seasoning.

Shape into balls. Make large meatballs to be served for dinner or small meatballs for the smörgåsbord.

Heat some of the margarine or butter in a skillet. When the foam subsides, add 10 to 15 meatballs. Cook over moderate heat until the meatballs are beautifully brown and cooked through. Transfer to a serving dish and keep hot while cooking the remaining meatballs. Serve with boiled potatoes, lingonberry preserve and a tossed salad.

Meat Loaf
Köttfärslimpa

Follow the recipe for meatballs. Shape mixture into a loaf and place on a buttered baking dish. Brush with beaten egg and sprinkle with bread crumbs. Bake in 175°C oven for 30 to 45 minutes. Baste the loaf occasionally. Add a little water if necessary.

Serve with the juice, boiled potatoes, vegetables and lingonberry preserve.

Beef Patties with Onions
Pannbiff med lök

2 cold boiled potatoes
400 g (14 oz.) ground beef
salt, white pepper
1 to 2 dl light cream and water
2 to 4 large onions, sliced
2 tablespoons margarine or butter

Mash the potatoes and mix with the meat. Add salt, pepper, cream and water. Work the meat mixture smooth and shape to patties.

Heat a skillet with some of the margarine or butter. When the foam subsides, add the onions and cook over moderate heat until golden brown. Transfer the onions to a platter and keep hot.

Heat the remaining margarine or butter in the skillet and fry the patties over moderate heat until brown on both sides and cooked through. Remove the patties to a heated serving platter and spread the onions on top. Add a little water to the skillet, heat and stir.

Serve the patties with the pan juices, boiled or fried potatoes and vegetables.

Beef Patties à la Lindström
Biff à la Lindström

Follow the recipe for beef patties with onions but add 2 finely chopped small pickled beets, 2 tablespoons finely chopped onion and 2 tablespoons capers to the meat mixture.

Cabbage Rolls
Kåldolmar

1 small head white cabbage
water, salt

Filling
1 dl (½ cup) water
½ dl (¼ cup) regular white rice
3 dl (1½ cups) milk
350 g (about 12 oz.) ground beef
salt, white pepper
thyme
margarine or butter
water
1 dl (½ cup) light cream

Cut out part of the core and put the cabbage in salted boiling water. Cook, covered, till the leaves are slightly soft and easy to remove from the core. Peel off the leaves one by one and drain on a rack or towel. Trim the coarse center vein of each leaf.

To make the filling, bring the water to a boil. Add the rice and cook, covered, until the water is almost absorbed. Stir in the milk and cook till the mixture resembles a thin porridge. Cool. Mix with the meat and spices, add more milk if necessary.

Put a large tablespoonful of filling on each cabbage leaf. Fold the leaf around the filling and secure the roll with a toothpick.

Heat a skillet with a little margarine or butter. When the foam subsides, add a few rolls and brown them well all around over moderate heat. Transfer to a casserole.

When all the cabbage rolls are browned, add a little water or beef bouillon to the casserole, cover and let simmer for about 30 minutes. Add the cream and cook for another 15 minutes.

Serve with boiled potatoes and lingonberry preserve.

Onion, pickled beets and capers give beef patties á la Lindström their special flavour.

Swedish Hash
Pytt i panna

3 tablespoons margarine or butter
8 to 10 raw or boiled potatoes, peeled
    and cut in small cubes
2 onions, finely chopped
100 g (3½ oz.) smoked ham, cut in small
    cubes
4 dl (1¾ cups) boiled or roast beef, cut in
    small cubes
1 teaspoon salt
white pepper
finely chopped parsley
4 egg yolks

Heat a skillet with some of the margarine
or butter. When the foam subsides, add
the potato cubes and cook over moderate
heat till golden brown and tender. Remove
to a platter.

Add the remaining margarine or butter
to the skillet and cook the onions till soft
and translucent; mix with the potatoes.

Sauté the ham, add the beef and brown
it lightly. Return the potatoes and onion to
the skillet, mix well. Add salt and pepper
to taste, heat the hash thoroughly and
transfer to a heated platter.

Sprinkle with chopped parsley. Let the
egg yolks remain in the half shells and
press into the hash; every diner stirs an egg
yolk into his serving of hash.

1 kg (2 lb. 3 oz.) breast of veal
2 teaspoons salt
1 liter (4 cups) water
10 white peppercorns

Boiled Falu Sausage with Horseradish Sauce
Kokt falukorv med pepparrotssås

500 g (about 1 lb.) falu sausage
5 dl (2 cups) water
1 to 2 beef bouillon cubes
1 to 2 slices onion
parsley sprig

Sauce
2 tablespoons margarine or butter
3 to 4 tablespoons flour
3 dl (1½ cups) milk
½ to 1 dl (¼ to ½ cup) liquid from cooking
    the sausage
grated horseradish
salt, white pepper

Pull the skin off the sausage and place in a
saucepan. Add the water, bouillon cubes,
onion and parsley. Let simmer, covered,
till the sausage is thoroughly hot.

In a small saucepan, melt the margarine
or butter. Blend in the flour, then add the
milk and cooking liquid. Bring to a boil,
beating the sauce until smooth. Let the
sauce simmer for a few minutes and season
to taste with grated horseradish, salt and
pepper.

Serve the sausage with the sauce, boiled
potatoes and a tossed salad.

Boiled Pork Sausage
Kokt fläskkorv

about 800 g (about 1 lb. 12 oz.) pork
  sausage
4 to 5 whole allspice
½ to 1 bay leaf
water

Rinse the sausage and put in a wide sauce-pan. Add the spices and enough water to cover the sausage. Let simmer, uncovered, for 30 minutes. Carefully turn the sausage around once during this time.

Cut in thick slices and serve with mash-ed potatoes or rutabagas (swedes). Or serve with boiled potatoes and white sauce flavored with mustard, horseradish or parsley.

The same recipe may be used for *köttkorv* or meat sausage, *Värmland sausage* and *grynkorv*. Cook the latter two for 45 min-utes.

Pork Sauce from Småland
Smålandsdoppa

200 g (7 oz.) lightly salted side pork
margarine or butter
1 small onion, finely chopped
3 tablespoons flour
5 dl (2 cups) milk
salt, white pepper

Cut the pork in small cubes. Heat a skillet and brown the pork adding a little mar-garine or butter. Add the chopped onion and cook for a few minutes together with the pork. Sprinkle with the flour and gradually add the milk. Cook the sauce for a few minutes and season to taste with salt and pepper.

Serve with potatoes boiled in their jackets.

Fried Pork with Onion Sauce
Stekt fläsk med löksås

400 g (14 oz.) lightly salted side pork
margarine or butter

Sauce
1—2 large onions, finely chopped
2 tablespoons flour
4 dl (1¾ cups) milk
salt, white pepper

Cut the pork in slices and fry in hot skillet adding a little margarine or butter; cook for 2 to 3 minutes on each side depending on how crisp you like your pork. Transfer to a platter and keep hot.

Sauté the chopped onion in a saucepan in lightly brown margarine or butter. Stir in the flour and then the milk. Blend well and let the sauce cook for a few minutes, it should be quite thick. Add salt and pepper to taste.

Serve the pork with the sauce, boiled potatoes and vegetables.

Swedish Steak with Onion
Svensk biff med lök

3 tablespoons margarine or butter
4 large onions, sliced
4 slices sirloin or top round of beef
    (about 500 g or 1 lb.)
salt, white pepper
water

Heat a skillet with some of the margarine or butter. When the foam subsides, add the onions. Lower the heat and cook until the onions are golden brown and tender. Remove to a platter and keep hot.

Pound the meat lightly with the back of your hand. Heat the remaining margarine or butter in the skillet and fry the steaks for about 3 minutes on each side. Season with salt and pepper and remove the steaks to a heated serving platter. Spread the fried onions on top.

Add a little water to the skillet, heat and stir. Serve the steaks at once with the pan juices, boiled, baked or fried potatoes and tossed salad.

Veal in Dill Sauce
Dillkött

1 kg (2 lb. 3 oz.) breast of veal
2 teaspoons salt
1 liter (4 cups) water
10 white peppercorns
3 cloves
1 bay leaf
1 carrot, sliced
1 onion
dill sprigs

Sauce
2 tablespoons margarine or butter
3 tablespoons flour
3 dl (1½ cups) liquid from cooking the veal
1 dl (½ cup) light cream + 1 egg yolk
salt, white pepper
finely chopped dill
fresh lemon juice

Put the meat in a saucepan, add the salt and enough water to cover. Bring to a boil. Remove the scum on the surface and lower the heat. Add the spices, cover and simmer for 1 hour. Then add the carrot, onion and dill sprigs. Let simmer for another 20 minutes. Remove the meat, cut in serving pieces and keep hot. Strain the cooking liquid.

In a small saucepan, melt the margarine or butter. Blend in the flour. Add the cooking liquid and bring to a boil, beating the sauce until smooth. Let cook for a few minutes. Remove from heat and beat in the cream mixed with the egg yolk. Season the sauce with salt, pepper, dill and lemon juice. Pour it over the meat or serve it separately. Serve with boiled potatoes or rice.

Veal in dill sauce.

Swedish Beef Stew
Kalops

1 kg (2 lb. 3 oz.) beef with bones or 600 g
    (1 lb. 5 oz.) boneless beef: rib, rump,
    brisket or bottom round
3 tablespoons margarine or butter
3 tablespoons flour
1½ teaspoons salt
2 onions, sliced
1 bay leaf
10 whole allspice
4 to 5 dl (1¾ to 2 cups) water

Cut the meat in large cubes. Heat the
margarine or butter in a heavy saucepan.
When the foam subsides, add the meat and
brown it well on all sides. Sprinkle with
the flour and salt. Stir the meat. Add the
onions, bay leaf, allspice and water. Cover
and simmer till tender, 1½ to 2 hours.

    Serve with boiled potatoes, pickled
beets and tossed salad.

Variation: When the meat has cooked 1
hour, add 2 sliced carrots and 2 leeks cut
in pieces.

    The stew may also be prepared with *elk*
or *reindeer* meat. Prepare *veal stew* the
same way but use half the allspice and bay
leaf.

Beef Roulades
Oxrulader

8 slices (about 600 g or about 1 lb.)
    boneless beef: sirloin or top round

1 teaspoon salt
white pepper
2 tablespoons margarine or butter
1 dl (½ cup) water

Filling
8 Swedish anchovy fillets
2 tablespoons finely chopped onion

Sauce
1 to 1½ tablespoon flour
2 dl cream

Sprinkle the meat with salt and pepper.
Put one anchovy fillet and a little chopped
onion on each slice and roll it up. Secure
the roulades with toothpicks.

    Heat a skillet with the margarine or
butter. When the foam subsides, add the
roulades and brown them well on all sides.
Add the water and cover. Simmer for
about 1 hour or till tender. Then remove
the roulades and make a sauce by adding
the flour mixed with a little cream to a
smooth paste. Add the rest of the cream.
Let the sauce cook for a few minutes and
return the roulades.

    Serve the roulades with the pan juices or
sauce, boiled or fried potatoes, vegetables,
lingonberry preserve and cucumber salad.

Sailor's Beef
Sjömansbiff

400 to 500 g (14 oz. to about 1 lb.)
    boneless beef: rib, rump or top round
3 tablespoons margarine or butter

1½ teaspoons salt
white pepper
2 large onions, sliced
10 to 12 potatoes, peeled and sliced
3 dl (1½ cups) beer or water

Cut the meat in slices. Heat a skillet with some of the margarine or butter. When the foam subsides, add the meat and brown on both sides. Season with salt and pepper. Brown the onions in the remaining margarine or butter.

Put the meat, onions and potatoes in layers in an oven-to-table casserole; the first and last layer should be potatoes. Sprinkle a little salt on the potatoes. Add beer or water, cover and let simmer for about 1 to 1½ hours.

Roast Lamb
Lammstek

1 kg (2 lb. 3 oz.) lamb roast
1½ teaspoons salt
white pepper
1 garlic clove
parsley sprig

Sauce
4 dl (1¾ cups) pan juices
2 tablespoons flour
cream
salt, white pepper

Place the roast, fat side up, on a rack in a roasting pan. Rub with salt and pepper. Insert the garlic clove and parsley sprig

close to the bone. Roast in a 175°C oven for little less than 2 hours. When a meat thermometer is used, roast until it reads 72 to 80°C. Allow the roast to rest on top of the stove for 10 minutes before carving.

Dilute the pan juice with hot water to make 4 dl. Bring to a boil. Stir in the flour mixed with a little cream to a smooth paste. Beat until smooth and let the sauce cook for a few minutes. Season to taste with salt and white pepper.

Game Casserole with Red Wine
Viltgryta med rödvin

400 g (14 oz.) boneless meat of elk,
**   venison or reindeer**
2 tablespoons flour
1 teaspoon salt
white pepper
3 tablespoons margarine or butter
2 carrots, sliced
1 onion, chopped
3 to 4 dl (1½ to 1¾ cups) red wine

Cut the meat in cubes and dip in flour mixed with salt and pepper. Heat a skillet with the margarine or butter. When the foam subsides, add the meat and cook until browned on all sides. Add the carrots, onion and wine. Simmer, covered, till the meat is tender.

Serve with rice and a green salad.

Reindeer Casserole
Renskavpanna

1 pkg frozen sliced reindeer meat
2 tablespoons margarine or butter
2 onions, finely chopped
1 teaspoon salt
white or black pepper
1 to 2 dl (½ to about 1 cup) light cream
1 to 2 teaspoons prepared mustard
finely chopped parsley

Heat a skillet with the margarine or butter. When the foam subsides, add the frozen meat. Gradually separate the meat slices as they cook. Fry until nicely browned. Add the chopped onions and cook together with the meat for a few minutes. Season with salt and pepper, then stir in the cream and mustard. Simmer for a few minutes.

Sprinkle with chopped parsley and serve hot with boiled potatoes and vegetables.

Roast Saddle of Reindeer
Rensadel

5 to 6 servings

1 saddle of reindeer, about 1½ kg
    (3 lb. 5 oz.)
2 teaspoons salt
white pepper

Sauce
3½ dl (about 1½ cups) pan drippings
    mixed with beef bouillon (cube)
2 tablespoons flour

½—1 dl (¼—½ cup) light cream
salt, white pepper
blue cheese
red currant jelly

If frozen, thaw the saddle so that the membranes and small silvery sinews can be removed. Rub with salt and pepper, then place the saddle on a rack in a roasting pan. Roast in a 175°C oven for 1½ to 2 hours. When a meat thermometer is used, roast till it reads 72 to 78°C. Allow the roast to rest on top of the stove for 10 minutes. Loosen the meat, carve in slices and put back on the saddle.

Add a little hot water to the roasting pan and stir to dissolve the pan drippings. Mix with beef bouillon to make 3½ dl (1½ cups). Bring to a boil in a small saucepan and stir in the flour mixed with the cream to a smooth paste. Let the sauce cook for a few minutes, beating until smooth. Season to taste with salt, pepper, blue cheese or red currant jelly.

Put the saddle on a serving platter and surround it with green beans and chestnut purée or tomato halves filled with pickled onions. Serve the sauce apart.

Saddle of venison or *lamb* may be cooked and served in the same way.

Roast saddle of reindeer.

Pot Roast
Grytstek

2 tablespoons margarine or butter
1 kg (2 lb. 3 oz.) rump or top round of
    beef, elk, reindeer, veal or pork
1½ to 2 teaspoons salt
white or black pepper
1 bay leaf
water

Sauce
4 dl (1¾ cups) pan juices mixed with
    cream
2 tablespoons flour
salt, white pepper

Heat the margarine or butter in a heavy
pot. When the foam subsides, add the
meat and brown it well all around. Season
with salt and pepper. Add the bay leaf and
a little hot water, cover and let the roast
cook over low heat: 1½ to 2 hours for beef,
elk and reindeer, 1 hour for pork and veal.
Baste the roast now and then, adding more
water if necessary. Remove the roast and
allow to rest for 10 minutes before carving.

   Mix the pan juices with cream to make
4 dl. Add the flour stirred with a little
cream to a smooth paste. Bring to a boil,
beating the sauce until smooth. Let cook
for a few minutes. Season the sauce with
salt and pepper to taste.

   Serve the roast with the sauce, boiled
potatoes, vegetables, red currant jelly and
pickles.

Roast Goose
Stekt gås

8 to 10 servings

1 goose (about 5 kg or 11 lb.)
1 lemon, cut in wedges
salt, white pepper
(ginger)
water

Stuffing
4 apples, peeled and cut in half
200 g (7 oz.) prunes

Sauce
4 dl (1¾ cups) pan juices or chicken
    bouillon
flour or arrowroot

Remove the intestines and rinse well. Pull
out the large sinews from the legs of the
goose. Rub it inside and out with lemon,
salt, white pepper and, if desired, ginger.
Stuff the goose with apples and prunes,
truss and place it, breast up, on a rack in a
shallow roasting pan. Roast in a 175°C
oven for 2½ to 3 hours.

   Test the goose by piercing the leg with a
toothpick; if the juice that runs out is clear
and colorless, the goose is done. For a nice
crisp skin, baste the goose with a few
tablespoons cold water and set the oven
door ajar the last 15 minutes of roasting
time.

   Pour the pan drippings into a saucepan
and skim off most of the fat. Add a little
water to the roasting pan and scrape to
dissolve any browned bits sticking to the
bottom; mix this with the pan drippings.

Bring to a boil and, if desired, make a gravy by adding a little flour or arrowroot.

Scoop out the filling and discard. Loosen the legs. Carve the breast meat in oblique slices and put back on the goose so that it looks whole.

Serve with boiled potatoes, red cabbage, stewed prunes and apple halves. The apples may be filled with orange mandarins and raisins that have been marinated in vinegar dressing.

Fried Chicken
Stekt kyckling

1 broiler chicken
50 g (about 2 oz.) margarine or butter
2 to 3 teaspoons curry powder or paprika
½ to 1 teaspoon salt

If frozen, thaw the chicken. Cut in half or in serving pieces.

Melt the margarine or butter in a skillet, stir in the curry powder or paprika. When the foam subsides, add the chicken and fry until nicely browned all around. Sprinkle with salt. Cover and cook over low heat on top of the stove or in a 175°C oven for 30 minutes.

Serve the chicken hot or cold with a tossed salad.

Chicken Casserole with Mushrooms
Kycklinggryta med champinjoner

1 broiler chicken
200 g (7 oz.) fresh mushrooms or
    one ¼-can mushrooms
margarine or butter
1½ to 2 tablespoons flour
1½ teaspoons salt
white or black pepper
2½ to 3 dl (1¼ to 1½ cups) chicken or
    beef bouillon (cube)
1 pkg frozen green beans

If frozen, thaw the chicken. Cut in serving pieces.

Trim and slice the fresh mushrooms; drain canned mushrooms. Heat a skillet with a little margarine or butter and sauté the mushrooms. Transfer to a casserole.

Dip the chicken into the flour mixed with salt and pepper. Heat the skillet adding a little more margarine or butter. When the foam subsides, add the chicken and brown well on all sides. Remove the chicken to the casserole and pour in the bouillon. Cover and let simmer for 10 minutes. Add the beans and cook for another 10 minutes.

Ovenbaked Christmas Ham
Ugnsbakad julskinka

3 to 5 kg (6 lb. to 11 lb.) lightly salted ham

Glaze
1 egg yolk
½ tablespoon sugar
2 to 3 tablespoons prepared Swedish mustard
2 to 3 tablespoons fine dry bread crumbs

Place the ham, rind up, on a rack in a roasting pan lined with aluminum foil. Insert a meat thermometer into the thickest part of the ham. Bake in a 150°C oven for 60—75 minutes/kg or till the thermometer reads 75°C.

Remove the rind and brush the top of the ham with the egg yolk, sugar and mustard stirred together. Sprinkle with bread crumbs. Bake in a 225°C oven until golden brown.

Garnish the ham with kale, prunes and an apple or orange. Serve cold cut in thin slices.

The ham may be baked wrapped in aluminum foil; then use a 175°C oven. Lightly smoked ham may be prepared in the same way.

Pork Roll
Fläskrulad

1 kg (2 lb.) fresh lean side pork
1 teaspoon white peppercorn
1 teaspoon whole allspice
2 teaspoons salt

water or stock
1 tablespoon salt
8 whole allspice
8 white peppercorn
1 bay leaf

Spread out the meat on a chopping-board. Cut the pork into two halves horizontally, but do not cut quite through. The halves should hang together at one side.

Crush the spices and mix with the salt. Sprinkle over the entire surface. Roll the meat tightly like a jelly roll. The rind should be on the outer side. Use string and tie the roll. Transfer the roll to a saucepan and pour over water or stock. Add salt and spices and bring to a boil. Simmer, covered, for about 2 hours.

Remove and place the roll on platter covered with a cutting board. Store in cold place for at least 10 hours. Serve sliced on the *julbord* with pickled beets or in the *doppa*.

Boneless rib from *veal* or *lamb* may be used instead of pork. Decrease the cooking time.

Spare Ribs
Revbensspjäll

1 kg (2 lb. 3 oz.) spare ribs

Seasonings
1 teaspoon salt
1 teaspoon ginger
1 pinch white pepper

or
2 dl (about 1 cup) chili sauce
½ dl (¼ cup) finely chopped onion
2 crushed garlic cloves
juice of ½ orange
2 tablespoons red wine vinegar
2 tablespoons oil
1 teaspoon prepared mustard
½ teaspoon salt
½ teaspoon freshly ground white pepper
1 teaspoon Worchestershire sauce

Rub the meat with the first spice mixture
or beat together the ingredients for the
second spice mixture and brush the meat.
Place it on a rotating spit or put the meat,
fat side up, on a rack in a shallow roasting
pan. Broil for 1 to 1½ hours. Or roast for
about 1½ hours in a 175°C oven; turn the
meat over once.

Dilute the pan drippings with a little
water, add salt and pepper to taste. If
desired, make a gravy by adding 2 tablespoons flour stirred with water to a smooth
paste. Cook the sauce for a few minutes.

Cut the meat in serving pieces and serve
with the pan juices or gravy, boiled potatoes, apple sauce and, if desired, brussels
sprouts or red cabbage.

Jellied Veal
Kalvsylta

1 kg (2 lb.) veal neck or veal breast
1 kg (2 lb.) veal shank or pork shank
1½ liter (6 cups) water
1 tablespoon salt
¼ teaspoon white pepper
¼ teaspoon ginger

Place the meat in a large saucepan and
pour the water over. Bring to a boil and
skim well. Simmer on low heat until meat
is tender, about 2 hours. Remove the
meat, and let cool.

Pick the meat from the bones and cut in
fine cubes or grind it.

Boil down the stock, strain and season
with salt, white pepper and ginger. Add
the meat and bring to a boil. Pour the
mixture into a large mold. Let cool and
chill in refrigerator.

Serve sliced with pickled beets.

Liver Pâté
Leverpastej

Makes 1,4 kg or 3 lb. 1 oz.

500 g (about 1 lb.) pork fat
500 g (about 1 lb.) pork liver
4 anchovy fillets
1 small onion, finely chopped
50 g (about 2 oz.) margarine or butter
¼ teaspoon white pepper
½ teaspoon salt
1 to 2 tablespoons potato flour
3 eggs
4 dl (1¾ cups) light cream

Cut part of the fat in very thin slices and line the bottom of a large loaf pan. Grease the sides.

Grind the liver, remaining fat and anchovies twice in meat grinder.

Sauté the chopped onion in the margarine or butter. Let cool and add to the liver mixture together with the spices. Work in the flour and eggs. Gradually add the cream and work the mixture till smooth and well blended. Pour a sample into a small tart pan and cook in saucepan with boiling water. If too soft, add more flour; if to firm, add more cream to the liver mixture.

Fill the loaf pan to ¾ with the mixture, cover with aluminum foil or greaseproof paper. Put the pan in a larger pan filled with hot water. Bake in a 200 to 225°C oven for 1½ hours.

If two smaller pans are used, bake for 1 hour only. Let the pâté cool before unmolding.

Pork Sausage
Fläskkorv

Makes about 5 kg or 11 lb.

3 kg (about 7 lb.) lean pork
1 kg (2 lb. 3 oz.) pork fat
1½ dl (¾ cup) potato flour
2½ tablespoons salt
1 tablespoon sugar
½ tablespoon white pepper
½ tablespoon ginger
1½ to 2 liter (6 to 8 cups) water or pork bouillon

sausage casings

Salt mixture
2 dl (about 1 cup) salt
1 dl (about ½ cup) sugar
2 tablespoons saltpeter

Grind the pork and fat twice in meat grinder. Stir in the flour and spices. Work the mixture well, gradually adding the liquid. Fill sausage casings loosely with the mixture. Rub with the salt mixture. Store in freezer or brine.

Liver paté

Pancakes and Waffles

S wedish pancakes come in two sizes: there are
the large thin pancakes or *tunnpannkakor*
baked on a griddle and the small *plättar* cooked in
the special *plättpanna*, a cast iron pan with seven
shallow depressions. Made from the same kind of
batter they are both favorite desserts of the
Swedes. They are also an integral part of the
traditional Thursday supper which includes pea
soup followed by pancakes and blueberry, raspberry, lingonberry or cloudberry preserve.

Crêpes

Makes about 12 crêpes

2 eggs
¾ dl (½ cup) flour
3 dl (1½ cups) light cream
½ teaspoon salt
2 tablespoons melted margarine or butter
(2 tablespoons grated cheese)

Creamed shellfish
2 tablespoons margarine or butter
4 tablespoons flour
4 dl (1¾ cups) liquid (cream mixed with
    milk or liquid from the canned shellfish)
½ to 1 teaspoon salt
white pepper
1 can lobster, crab or clams (100 g or
    3½ oz.) or 1 pkg frozen shrimps (200 g
    or 7 oz.)

Beat together the eggs, flour and half of
the cream to a smooth batter. Add the
remaining cream, salt, and melted margarine or butter.

Heat a crêpe pan with a little margarine
or butter. When hot, remove from heat
and add about 2 tablespoons batter. Tilt
the pan to spread the batter in a thin layer.
Cook over medium-high heat for about 1
minute, then remove the crêpe. Stir the
batter now and then.

Put a string of creamed shellfish on the
unbaked side of each crêpe and roll it up.
Serve at once. Or serve the crêpes au
gratin: put the rolls in a buttered baking
dish and sprinkle with the cheese. Bake in
a 250°C oven until the cheese is a golden
brown.

To make the creamed shellfish, melt the
margarine or butter in a saucepan. Stir in
the flour. Add the liquid and bring to a
boil, beating until smooth. Let cook for 3
to 5 minutes. Season to taste with salt and
pepper. Remove from heat and fold in the
shellfish.

Variation: Instead of shellfish, filling may
be made of mushrooms, asparagus or
sweetbread.

Thin Pancakes with Pork
Tunna fläskpannkakor

2 eggs
3 dl (1½ cups) flour
6 dl (about 3 cups) milk
(½ teaspoon salt)
200 g (7 oz.) lightly salted lean side pork
margarine or butter

Beat together the eggs, flour and half of
the milk to a smooth batter. Add the
remaining milk and, if desired, salt.

Cut the pork in small cubes; cook in hot
skillet until brown and mix with the pancake batter.

Heat a pancake griddle with a little
margarine or butter. Add enough batter to
cover the griddle in a thin layer. Cook over
moderate heat for a couple of minutes or
till set on the surface, then turn the pancake over. Cook the other side for about 1
minute. Try to get the same amount of
pork in each pancake.

Serve hot with lingonberry preserve.

Swedish Pancakes
Plättar och pannkakor

1 dl (½ cup) flour
3 dl (1½ cups) rich milk or 1½ dl (¾ cup)
   water and 1½ dl whipping cream
3 eggs
1 pinch salt
3 tablespoons melted margarine or butter

Beat together the flour and half of the milk, or the water, to a smooth batter. Add the eggs, remaining milk, or cream, salt and melted margarine or butter. Beat until well blended.

To make small pancakes or *plättar*, heat a *plättpanna* with a little margarine or butter in each depression. When hot, add about 1 tablespoon batter to each section and cook over medium-high heat for 1 minute or till the surface has set and the bottom is a golden brown. Use a small spatula and turn the pancakes over; cook the other side for about half a minute. If possible, serve the pancakes at once. Continue cooking without adding more margarine or butter to the pan. Stir the batter now and then.

To make the larger pancakes, heat a griddle with a little margarine or butter. Remove from heat, add about ½ dl batter and tilt the pan to spread the batter in a thin layer. Cook over medium-high heat for 1 to 2 minutes, then use a long narrow spatula and turn the pancake over. Cook the other side for about half a minute.

Serve the pancakes at once, or stack them on a plate and keep hot over a pan with boiling water.

If desired, make a *pancake tårta* by stacking the pancakes with apple sauce or other fruit preserve between the layers. Let cool and spread the top with whipped cream. Serve cut in wedges.

Crisp Waffles
Frasvåfflor

Makes 6 to 8 large waffles

2½ dl (1¼ cups) flour
1½ dl (¾ cup) cold water
2½ dl (1¼ cups) whipping cream

Beat together the flour and water. When smooth, add about ½ dl (¼ cup) cream. Whip the remaining cream until thick and fold into the batter. Heat the waffle iron; do not grease. Cook each waffle until crisp and golden brown.

Serve the waffles with strawberry, raspberry or cloudberry preserve and whipped cream or vanilla ice cream.

Delicious crisp waffles with whipped cream and fruit preserves.

Pastries and Desserts

The traditional Swedish coffee table used to include a sweet yeast bread, one or two plain cakes, numerous cookies and a fancy filled cake called *tårta*. Still a common form of entertaining, the coffee party today is a much less elaborate affair that may feature just one or two baked items, maybe the popular *sockerkaka* (sponge cake) and a few cookies. On festive occasions, such as birthdays and namedays, a tårta is a must.

Fresh fruit and ice cream are maybe the two most common desserts in Sweden. Swedish apples are delicious and so are the pears, red and black currants, gooseberries and strawberries grown in the country. Among the wild berries of prime importance are lingonberries, blueberries and cloudberries.

The cloudberry, an exquisite fruit from the marshes of northern Sweden, looks somewhat like a yellow raspberry but has a distinctive delightful flavor of its own. Vanilla ice cream with a topping of fresh or frozen cloudberries, or cloudberry preserve, is truly delicious. Cloudberry preserve is also served with pancakes and waffles or used as filling for tårta and almond tarts. A good and easy dessert may be made from sliced sockerkaka topped with whipped cream and cloudberries.

Sweet Yeast Bread
Vetebröd

Makes 4 loaves or about 40 buns

150 to 200 g (5 to 7 oz.) margarine or
   butter
½ liter (2 cups) milk
50 to 75 g (2 to 2¼ oz.) yeast
½ teaspoon salt
1½ dl (¾ cup) sugar
(1 teaspoon ground cardamom)
1½ liter or 900 g (6 cups or 2 lb.) flour

Fillings
 I. 100 g (3½ oz.) margarine or butter
    ¾ dl (½ cup) sugar
    ½ tablespoon cinnamon or ground
       cardamom
II. 100 g (3½ oz.) margarine or butter
    ¾ dl (½ cup) sugar
    50 g (about 2 oz.) ground nuts

Garnish
beaten egg
(pearl sugar)

In a saucepan, melt the margarine or butter. Remove from heat and add the milk. Crumble the yeast into a large mixing bowl, add the salt, sugar, cardamom and milk mixture. Stir in most of the flour and work the dough until smooth and shiny. Cover and leave to rise for 10 minutes in the mixing bowl.

Turn the dough onto pastry board and knead it well. Divide in parts and shape into buns, loaves, etc. Let rise on baking sheet until double in size. Brush with beaten egg and, if desired, sprinkle with pearl sugar. Bake the buns in a 225 to 250°C oven for 5 to 10 minutes; bake the loaves in a 200 to 225°C oven for 15 to 20 minutes.

Plain Loaves Släta längder

Divide the dough in 4 parts. Roll out each part into a rectangle about 20 by 35 cm. Spread with the desired filling. Roll up from the long side and place the roll on baking sheet. If desired, score each loaf with a sharp knife at 1 cm intervals. Cover with a cloth and let rise, then brush with beaten egg and bake.

Twisted Loaves Vridna längder

Roll out, fill and roll up the dough as for plain loaves. Cut each roll in half lengthwise, then twist the two halves together. Let rise, brush with beaten egg and bake.

Butter Cake Butterkaka

Roll out, fill and roll up the dough as for plain loaves. Cut each roll in 3 cm thick slices and place, cut side up, in a well buttered and floured cake pan. Place the slices about 2 cm apart. Let rise, brush with beaten egg and bake.

Small Buns Småbullar

Roll out, fill and roll up the dough as for plain loaves. Cut each roll in slices 4 cm thick; place, cut side up, on baking sheet. Let rise, brush with beaten egg and, if desired, sprinkle with pearl sugar. Bake.

Saffron Buns
Saffransbröd

1 recipe sweet yeast bread
1 egg
1 g (⅓ oz) ground saffron

Garnish
raisins

Prepare the dough as for sweet yeast bread; take the larger amount of margarine or butter. Before adding the flour, stir in 1 beaten egg and 1 g ground saffron dissolved in a little milk. Shape the dough into buns, loaves or rounds.

To make the special Christmas buns or *julkusar*, pinch off small pieces of the dough and shape into 1 cm wide strips, about 12 cm long. Put two strips together side by and curl in the ends. Stick a raisin into each curl.

Let rise, brush with beaten egg and bake.

Prepare the dough and shape into 15 to 20 round balls; place on baking sheet. Let rise, brush with beaten egg and bake in a 250°C oven for 5 to 10 minutes. Let cool covered with a cloth.

Cut a lid off the top of each bun. Fill with a piece of almond paste and cover with whipped cream. Put the lid on top of the cream. If desired, dust with icing sugar.

Or cut a lid and scoop out the inside of each bun. Mix the breadcrumbs with the whipped cream, chopped nuts and sugar; return to the bun and replace the lid. Powder with icing sugar.

Fat Tuesday Buns
Fettisdagsbullar, semlor

½ recipe sweet yeast bread

Filling
2 dl (about 1 cup) whipping cream
200 g (7 oz.) almond paste or 3 dl
    (1½ cups) whipping cream
1½ dl (¾ cup) hazelnuts, chopped
3 tablespoons sugar

Saffron buns, sweet yeast bread flavoured with saffron, belong to Christmas and especially Lucia Day celebrations in December.

Quick Rolls
Hastbullar

Makes 16 to 20 rolls

5 dl (2 cups) or 300 g flour
2½ teaspoons baking powder
1 dl (½ cup) sugar
1 teaspoon ground cardamom or 2 to 3
   grated bitter almonds
100 g (3½ oz.) margarine or butter
1 egg
2 dl (about 1 cup) milk
1 dl (½ cup) raisins, 2 to 3 tablespoons
   chopped candled citron, 8 to 10 chop-
   ped candled cherries or 50 g (about
   2 oz.) chopped chocolate

Garnish
beaten egg
pearl sugar
chopped almonds

Rub the margarine or butter into the dry
ingredients mixed together. Beat together
the egg and milk, stir into the flour mixture. Add raisins, citron, cherries or chocolate, if desired. Quickly work the dough
together and drop into paper cups.

Brush with beaten egg and sprinkle with
pearl sugar and chopped almonds. Bake in
a 200 to 225°C oven for about 10 minutes.

Danish Pastry
Danska wienerbröd

Makes 35 pastries.

40 g (1¾ oz.) yeast
⅓ teaspoon salt
2 tablespoons sugar
1 egg
2½ dl (1¼ cups) milk
8½ dl (3¾ cups, about 500 g or 1 lb. 1 oz.)
   flour
250 g (8½ oz.) margarine or butter

Vanilla filling
2 dl (about 1 cup) milk
2 tablespoons flour
1 egg yolk
1 tablespoon sugar
2 teaspoons vanilla sugar

Nut filling
50 g (about 2 oz.) ground nuts
¾ dl (½ cup) sugar
50 g (about 2 oz.) margarine or butter

Garnish
1 egg
blanched almonds, chopped or sliced

Crumble the yeast into a large mixing
bowl, add the salt and sugar. Beat together
the egg and milk, add to the yeast. Stir in
flour to make the dough firm enough and
work it smooth and shiny. Turn it onto a
pastry board and knead well.

Roll out the dough to a rectangle about
1½ cm thick. Cut the margarine or butter
in slices and place on ⅔ of the dough; note
that it must not be placed too close to the

edge of the dough. Fold the dough in three starting with the plain part. Turn the dough ¼ turn; the "back" of the dough should be facing you. Press lightly with a rolling pin and roll again out the dough to a rectangle. Fold in three.

If smeary, let the dough rest in refrigerator for 15 minutes. Turn the dough as before, roll out and fold in three. If desired, chill the dough before rolling out and folding one more time.

The dough is now ready to be used for Crescents, Combs and Vienna Rolls. Always let the pastries rise slowly on the baking sheet. Brush with beaten egg and bake in a 250 to 275°C oven for 5 to 8 minutes.

To make the vanilla filling, mix all the ingredients except vanilla sugar in a saucepan and bring to a simmer, stirring continuously. Let cool and stir in the vanilla.

To make the nut filling, work together the nuts, sugar and margarine or butter.

Combs
Kammar

1 recipe Danish Pastry

Roll out the dough to a rectangle ½ cm thick and 30 cm wide. Spread with nut filling or butter. Fold the dough in three lengthwise. Cut in slices 4 to 5 cm thick. Make a few slits at one side of each pastry, bend it a little and place on baking sheet.

Leave to rise slowly. Brush with beaten egg and sprinkle with chopped or sliced blanched almonds before baking.

Crescents
Gifflar

1 recipe Danish Pastry

Roll out the dough to ½ cm thickness. Cut with a pastry wheel or knife in 10 cm squares, cut these in two diagonally. Spread with butter or any of the fillings. Roll up from the wide base. Bend the pastries slightly and place on baking sheet. Leave to rise slowly, brush with beaten egg and bake.

If desired, spread the pastries when cool with icing sugar stirred with water to a thin glaze.

Vienna Rolls
Wienerrullar

1 recipe Danish Pastry

Roll out the dough to a rectangle about ½ cm thick and 25 cm wide. Spread with nut filling along the edges and roll up the dough from both of the long sides. Cut in 1 cm thick slices across and place on baking sheet. Leave to rise slowly and bake without brushing with egg.

If desired, paint the pastries after baking with water mixed with sugar.

111

Crullers
Klenäter

Makes about 30

4 egg yolks
50 g (¼ cup) sugar
¼ teaspoon salt
1 tablespoon aquavit or cognac
grated rind of 1 lemon
2 tablespoons softened butter
100 g (1 cup) flour

For cooking
vegetable shortening or oil

Garnish
sugar

Stir together the egg yolks, sugar, salt, aquavit and lemon rind. Add the butter and flour; quickly work the dough together. Chill for 2 hours.

Roll out the dough on lightly floured surface to little more than 3 mm thickness. Use a ruler and cut the dough with pastry wheel into strips, 3 by 10 cm, with slanted edges. Cut a 3 cm slit in center of each strip and pull one end through the slit.

Heat the fat in heavy-bottomed pan to 175°C. The fat should go about 8 cm deep. Cook a few crullers at a time until golden, about 1 minute. Drain on paper towel for a minute, then dip both sides in sugar.

Almond Tarts
Mandelmusslor

Makes about 35

1 dl (½ cup) sugar
200 g (7 oz.) margarine or butter
100 g (3½ oz.) almonds
5 bitter almonds
4 dl (1¾ cups) flour
2 tablespoons cornstarch

Stir the sugar and margarine or butter till light and fluffy. Grind the almonds. Work all the ingredients together and chill the dough for 1 hour or longer.

Coat well buttered, small, fluted tart pans with a thin layer of the dough; press with your thumbs. Bake in a 200°C oven for about 10 minutes. Let cool for a few minutes, then gently knock the tarts out of the pans.

Serve the cookies empty or filled with fruit and whipped cream.

Crullers and almond tarts filled with whipped cream and cloudberry preserve.

Oatmeal Wafers
Havreflarn

Makes about 30 cookies

75 g (2¼ oz.) **margarine or butter**
1 dl (½ cup) **oatmeal**
1 dl (½ cup) **flour**
1 dl (½ cup) **sugar**
2 tablespoons **light cream**
2 tablespoons **syrup**
¼ teaspoon **baking powder**

In a saucepan, melt the margarine or butter. Stir in the remaining ingredients. Drop the batter in teaspoonfuls wide apart on buttered cookie sheets. Bake in a 200°C oven for about 5 minutes. Let the cookies cool for about 1 minute, then remove from the cookie sheet.

If desired, drape the cookies over a rolling pin or similarly shaped object to harden and finish cooling.

Ginger Snaps
Pepparkakor

Makes about 500 cookies

3 dl (1½ cups) **syrup**
4 dl (1¾ cups) **sugar**
1½ tablespoons **ginger**
1½ tablespoons **cinnamon**
1 tablespoon **cloves**
350 g (12 oz.) **margarine or butter**
3 dl (1½ cups) **whipping cre**

about 2½ liter or 1½ kg (3 lb. 5 oz.) **flour**
1 tablespoon **baking soda**

Stir the syrup with sugar, spices and margarine or butter until well mixed. Whip the cream till frothy and stir into the batter, a little at a time. Dissolve the baking soda in a little water and add together with part of the flour. Cover the dough which should be quite firm, let stand till the following day.

Knead the dough, adding the remaining flour. Roll out a small part and bake a test cookie in a 175 to 200°C oven. If the cookie spreads, add a little more flour to the dough. Roll out the dough very thin and cut with cookie cutters into hearts, stars, pigs, etc. Let the cookies cool on the cookie sheet after baking.

The cookies may be decorated with white frosting made of sifted icing sugar stirred with egg white and a few drops vinegar or lemon juice to a thick smooth paste.

Sponge Cake
Sockerkaka

2 **eggs**
1½ to 2 dl (¾ to 1 cup) **sugar**
2 teaspoons **vanilla sugar or grated rind of ½ lemon**
3 dl (1½ cups) **flour**
2 teaspoons **baking powder**
50 g (about 2 oz.) **margarine or butter**
1 dl (½ cup) **milk**

Beat the eggs and sugar until pale and thick. Add the desired flavoring, flour and baking powder. Melt the margarine or butter and let cool; stir into the batter. Add milk, a little at a time. Mix well to a smooth batter. Pour into a buttered cake pan (1½ liter) that has been sprinkled with fine dry bread crumbs. Bake for about 45 minutes in a 175°C oven.

Princess Cake
Prinsesstårta

Makes about 20 servings

3 eggs
1½ dl (¾ cup) sugar
¾ dl (about ½ cup) flour
¾ dl (about ½ cup) potato flour
1 teaspoon baking powder

Filling
2 egg yolks
4 tablespoons sugar
2 teaspoons vanilla sugar
5 leaves gelatine or equivalent amount gelatine powder
4 dl (1¾ cups) whipping cream

Garnish
225 g (about 7 oz.) marzipan
or 175 g (about 6 oz.) almond paste, 1 dl (½ cup) powdered sugar and a little glucose (optional)
green food color
icing sugar

Beat the eggs and sugar until pale and thick. Mix the two kinds of flour and the baking powder; add to the egg batter. Blend well and pour the mixture into a buttered round cake pan (about 2 liter) that has been sprinkled with fine dry bread crumbs. Bake in a 175°C oven for 30 minutes. Unmold the cake and let cool. Split the cake horizontally in two parts.

Beat together the egg yolks and sugar for the filling. Whip the cream thick. Soak the gelatine leaves in water, wring them well and dissolve over heat. If gelatine powder is used, follow the directions on the package. Blend the gelatine with the egg mixture. Fold in the whipped cream. Let stand until almost set.

Put the two cake layers together with part of the filling between. Spread the remaining filling over the top and the sides of the cake which should be somewhat higher in center with sloping sides.

Work the marzipan smooth, or mix the almond paste with the sugar and, if desired, a little glucose. Add food color and blend well to a light green. Roll the marzipan between two sheets of lightly oiled wax paper or plastic foil into a circle large enough to cover the entire cake.

Remove the upper paper and turn the marzipan over the cake. Gently remove the second piece of paper. Press the marzipan close to the sides of the cake. Sift with icing sugar. Store the cake in refrigerator till serving time.

Red Currant Cake
Vinbärstårta

about 1 liter (4 cups) red currants
sugar
3 round cake layers
2 dl (about 1 cup) whipping cream

Mix the currants with sugar to taste; stir until slightly crushed. Put the cake layers together with the berries between. Whip the cream thick and spread on top. Garnish with nice clusters of red currants.

Swedish Apple Cake
Svensk äppelkaka

6 to 8 tart apples (about 600 g or 1 lb.
** 5 oz.)**
water
sugar to taste
or 4 dl (1¾ cups) lightly sweetened apple
** sauce**
2 to 3 dl (about 1 to 1½ cups) grated dry
** rye bread or finely crushed rusks or**
** bread crumbs**
sugar, cinnamon
50 g (about 2 oz.) margarine or butter

Peel the apples and cut in wedges. Cook, covered, in a little water with sugar until soft and mushy.

Brown the grated bread, crushed rusks or bread crumbs mixed with a little sugar and cinnamon in the margarine or butter.

Butter a baking dish or skillet well and cover with a layer of the bread crumbs.

Spread a layer of apple sauce on top, then another layer of bread crumbs and apple sauce. Finish with a layer of bread crumbs.

Bake in a 225°C oven for 25 to 35 minutes. Let the cake cool a little in the baking dish.

If desired, unmold the cake on a serving plate and garnish with sugar. Then cut thin strips of paper and put crosswise on top of the cake. Sift with icing sugar and carefully remove the strips.

Serve the apple cake with vanilla sauce or cream. Note that the cake need not be baked. Pack the browned bread crumbs and apple sauce in a dish. Let stand for 1 to 2 hours, then unmold.

Fyris Cake
Fyriskaka

125 g (4 oz.) margarine or butter
1½ dl (¾ cup) sugar
2 eggs
2½ dl (1¼ cups) flour
½ teaspoon baking powder
2 tablespoons light cream

Garnish
400 to 500 g (14 oz. to about 1 lb.) soft
** apples**
sugar to taste

Melt the margarine or butter. Let cool and stir with the sugar. Add the eggs, one at a time, then the flour, baking powder and cream. Pour the mixture into a buttered round baking dish or skillet (about 1½ liter) that has been sprinkled with fine dry bread crumbs.

Peel the apples and cut in thin wedges; stick these into the batter. Sprinkle with sugar on top. Bake for 30 minutes in a 200°C oven.

Cheese Cake from Småland
Småländsk ostkaka

Makes 10 to 12 servings

8 liter (about 2 gallons) milk
3½ dl (about 1½ cups) flour
2 tablespoons rennet
8 eggs
4 egg yolks
3½ dl (about 1½ cups) sugar
100 g (3½ oz.) chopped blanched almonds
1 liter (4 cups) milk mixed with light cream
½ liter (2 cups) whipping cream

Mix ½ liter (2 cups) milk with the flour and rennet. Heat the remaining milk to about 35°C, then add the flour mixture. Set aside until curdled or about 1 hour. Cut in large pieces and strain through a cloth. Spread the curds in a buttered baking dish (4 liter or about 1 gallon).

Beat together the eggs, egg yolks, sugar, almonds, milk and cream; pour the batter over the curds. Stir until well blended. Bake in a 175°C oven for about 1½ hours.

Serve warm with fruit preserve. Makes 10 to 12 servings.

Creamed Rice
Risgrynsgröt

5 dl (2 cups) water
1½ tablespoons margarine or butter
2 dl (about 1 cup) regular white rice
2 dl (about 1 cup) whipping cream
salt, sugar

In a large saucepan, bring the water to a boil. Add the rice and margarine or butter. Let simmer, covered, for 20 minutes without stirring. Stir in the whipped cream, let simmer for 3 to 4 minutes. Stir now and then. Season to taste with salt and sugar. If too thick, add a little milk.

For a version, not quite as rich substitute 2 dl (about 1 cup) nonfat dry milk stirred with 1 dl (½ cup) water for the cream. Add a little grated lemon rind.

Black Currant Mousse
Svartvinbärsfromage

3 egg yolks
1 dl (½ cup) sugar
½ liter (2 cups) black currants
4 soaked leaves gelatine or equivalent
   amount gelatine powder
3 egg whites

Beat the egg yolks and sugar till fluffy.
Mix with the berries. Dissolve the soaked
gelatine leaves over light heat. If gelatine
powder is used, follow the directions on
the package. Blend the gelatine with the
berry mixture.

   Beat the egg whites till stiff and fold into
the mixture. Spoon the mousse into serving glasses and garnish with black currants. Chill before serving.

Variation: Mix black or red currents with
whipped cream or stiffly beaten egg
whites. Add sugar to taste, chill and serve.

Berry Dessert
Bärkräm

½ liter (1 lb.) strawberries, raspberries,
   blueberries or gooseberries
1½ to 2 dl (½ to ¾ cup) sugar
3 tablespoons potato starch flour
4 dl (1½ cups) water

Trim berries if necessary. Place in a saucepan. Sprinkle with sugar and potato starch
flour, and pour over water. Bring to boiling point, stirring all time. Sprinkle with
sugar and let cool covered. Serve with milk
in soup plates.

Menu Suggestions

Luncheons

Thin Pancakes with Pork p. 103
Lingonberry Preserve and Coleslaw
★

Coffee

Grapefruit
★

Fried Plaice with Capers and Beets p. 75
Boiled Potatoes and Tossed Green Salad
★

Coffee and Fyris Cake p. 116

Fried Stromming p. 72
Mashed Potatoes and Shredded Carrots
★

Coffee

Suppers

Swedish Hash p. 88
★
Coffee and Ginger Snaps p. 114

Vegetable Soup p. 57
★
Cheesecake with Strawberry Preserve p. 117
or Swedish Pancakes
with Cloudberry Preserve p. 104

Meat Balls p. 85
Boiled Potatoes and Tossed Green Salad
Lingonberry Preserve
★
Berry Dessert p. 118

Dinners

Pickled Herring p. 65
★

Beef Patties with Onions p. 85
Boiled Potatoes, Cucumber Salad p. 52
★

Swedish Apple Cake p. 116 with Vanilla Ice Cream
or Vanilla Sauce

Three Small Sandwiches p. 44
★

Roast Saddle of Reindeer p. 94
Baked or Boiled Potatoes, Tossed Salad
★

Black Currant Mousse p. 118

Dinners

West Coast Salad p. 52
★

Roast Lamb p. 93
Hasselback Potatoes p. 60
Vegetables and Jelly or Pickles
★

Ice Cream with Fresh or Frozen Berries

Nettle or Spinach Soup p. 56
★

Ovenbaked Pike p. 81
Boiled Potatoes and Vegetables
★

Coffee with Almond Tarts filled with Fruit and
Whipped Cream p. 112

Suggestions for a Smörgåsbord

Pickled Herring p. 65 or Glassblower's Herring, p. 64
Boiled Potatoes
Buckling in Mustard Marinade, p. 72
Jansson's Temptation, p. 71
Liver Paté, p. 100
Fresh or Pickled Cucumber
Pork Roll, p. 98
Pickled Beets
Mushroom Omelette with Sausages, p. 62
Meat Balls, p. 85
Mixed Sallad
Butter, Rye Bread and Crispbread
Coffee and Sponge Cake, p. 114

Index

Register

128